# NINE LIVES

# NINE LIVES

*An anthology of poetry and prose*
*concerning* CATS

Compiled by
**Kenneth Lillington**

Illustrated by
**Maurice Wilson**

ANDRE DEUTSCH

First published 1977 by
André Deutsch Limited
105 Great Russell Street London WC1

Copyright © 1977 by Kenneth Lillington
All rights reserved

Printed in Great Britain by
Jolly & Barber Ltd, Rugby

ISBN 0 233 96927 6

To My Wife

*in love and friendship*

# Personal Acknowledgment

My grateful thanks are due to those friends and colleagues who suggested items for this anthology, and to my former student, Jane Lambert, for typing some of the manuscript.

# Contents

# Introduction

This anthology is for cat-lovers and even cat-haters (see Skelton's Curse for the murderous Gib). Here are cool cats, sharp cats, cynical cats, cats praised in their own right and cats who throw light on the meaning of existence, comic cats, cosseted cats, and even hell-cats, like Poe's Black Cat with its one red eye of fire. The Pathetic Fallacy weaves its way unashamedly through these pages, because, where cats are concerned, to deny the Pathetic Fallacy is even more fallacious than to subscribe to it. You can't treat a cat objectively without dwindling to a pedant. A cat is a cat is just not merely a cat. It is an object of worship or an agent of Satan or a symbol of sensuality or a surrogate for Woman, and you cannot divorce it from its mystery. It is the eternal contemporary, the one animal, unlike the servile dog or the exploited horse, who can sponge on the human race and keep its freedom. It has us where it wants us.

As for me, I have measured out my life with Kattomeat. Two cats currently have me in thrall. One is Floyd, an amiable tabby who has learned the art of deep relaxation and spends most of his life in a comatose heap on the Potterton boiler, edging further and further away from the hot pipe until he collapses between the boiler and the fridge, from where he extricates himself with difficulty and labour and climbs back up, with difficulty and labour hee. You will find some master-minds in the pages that follow, but Floyd, I am afraid, is not one of them. He cannot grasp even the immediately obvious. Having howled persistently at the door from outside, he will sit there and continue howling after the door is opened and he is urged to enter the house. He will howl at a cupboard supposing it to be the street door, or at the street door in the delusion that it is a cupboard full of food. He is then transfixed with dismay to find himself out in the street.

If Floyd is a C-stream cat, Pharaoh, the Russian Blue, has an honours degree; but he is very highly-strung, and is nonplussed by circumstances. He spins a dark web of suspicion round every situation. He approaches his food as though it were a land-mine, his elbows sticking up above his ears. He will not eat if anyone is in the room. If you want to make sure he is getting his food you must creep into the garden and watch him through the window. He sees devils and in the midst of social calm will take to sudden flight, his eyes black with terror. He understands human speech and can, I believe, read the labels on bottles, and whenever we want to give him a pill he will retreat to an inaccessible corner and sit erect and immobile, watching us steadily from clear, cold eyes.

Cats appear in their hundreds in children's books, but very few of them fit in with this intellectual lot. But there's one I must bring in – the glorious Korky, the cat of The Dandy. I could not include him in the main body of this anthology because his adventures are pictorial, but he deserves a special mention for his cheerful courage in calamity, and for that indefinable elan which makes for star quality.

He has an arch enemy, a brutal pug-faced fellow in a tiger-striped jersey, whose aim in life seems to be to humiliate and degrade him. It is this oaf who arranges planks through holes in fences (on the fulcrum principle) with buckets of whitewash on one end, so that when Korky steps on the other end the whitewash is flung all over him, and we see him submerged, with only holes for eyes staring out aghast; or fixes bricks under tophats, to kick which causes Korky such anguish that it radiates from his toe in zig-zag lines. Sometimes our hero is made a present of a handsome cake, which he invariably leaves (admittedly rather carelessly) on the windowsill of his house; and you may be sure that no sooner has he done so than the tiger-striped hooligan will rush up and snatch it, to go gambading off in disgusting exultation. Ah, but next we see Korky compounding a cake of his own, pouring in soot (from a bag marked 'soot') and glue (from a jar marked 'glue') and *this* he also places on the windowsill. Pug Face hastens to grab it, and we see him, finally, struggling in an obscene morass, while Korky winks to us gaily, inset in a little circle! In this age of anti-heroes he shows a spirit which might otherwise have died in the world.

I had at first intended to keep out the half-human hybrids, the cats who wear clothes or speak English, but the loss (The Cheshire Cat, Mehitabel, Lear's Pussy Cat and Tobermory) was too great. It seemed an easy matter to stick to the English language, but I could not resist putting in *Les Chats*, by Baudelaire, in the original, because it is the supreme cat poem, saying all that should be said about cats, and feline in its very sound.

Cats make us maudlin if we aren't careful, and I read many arch pieces that should never have seen the light of day, but the good things came in wonderful variety. Some authors treat the subject with a grin, some with a secret smile like the Mona Lisa, a few are quite serious and one or two are annoyed. Cats are exceedingly evasive and won't be classified, but they have their ups and downs like us, which enables me to group them For Better or For Worse; and I have managed to sort them out further into Reprobates, Mystics, a category of pieces that discuss their Nature, and a miscellany which I have entitled Strays. These Strays are by no means waifs. Most of them are doing fine. They simply do not fit into the other groups.

One notable omission is Kipling's *The Cat That Walked by Himself*. Its conclusion – that Three Proper Men Out of Five Will Throw Things at a Cat when They See One – revolts me, not so much for the ill-treatment of the cat, as for Kipling's idea of a man, with its subtle reek of sahib-mentality. Another is Swift's *The Widow and the Cat*, a political attack, not really about cats at all. Then there is a little piece by Walter Savage Landor, *A Quarrelsome Bishop:*

> To hide her ordure, claws the cat;
> You claw, but not to cover that.
> Be decenter, and learn at least
> One lesson from the cleanlier beast.

This is too quotable to be left unquoted, but I have left out of the body of the book pieces of this kind, where the cat and her claws are only brought in to scratch a human being.

# For Better

The cats in this section are, or are about to be, purring.
Cats fall on their feet, so this section is much the longest.
One or two of them experience the fell clutch of
circumstance, but prove too slippery for it. Cats know a
sucker when they see one, and this section leaves us in no
doubt as to why they condescend to live with us.

# Pangur Ban

I and Pangur Ban my cat
'Tis a like task we are at:
Hunting mice is his delight,
Hunting words I sit all night.

Better far than praise of men
'Tis to sit with book and pen;
Pangur bears me no ill-will,
He too plies his simple skill.

'Tis a merry thing to see
At our tasks how glad are we,
When at home we sit and find
Entertainment to our mind.

Oftentimes a mouse will stray
In the hero Pangur's way;
Oftentimes my keen thought set
Takes a meaning in its net.

'Gainst the wall he sets his eye
Full and fierce and sharp and sly;
'Gainst the wall of knowledge I
All my little wisdom try.

When a mouse darts from its den
O how glad is Pangur then!
O what gladness do I prove
When I solve the doubts I love!

So in peace our tasks we ply,
Pangur Ban, my cat, and I;
In our arts we find our bliss,
I have mine and he has his.

Practice every day has made
Pangur perfect in his trade;
I get wisdom day and night
Turning darkness into light.

# The Doctor and His Cat Hodge

I shall never forget the indulgence with which he treated Hodge, his cat: for whom he himself used to go out and buy oysters, lest the servants having that trouble should take a dislike to the poor creature. I am, unluckily, one of those who have an antipathy to a cat, so that I am uneasy when in the room with one; and I own, I frequently suffered a good deal from the presence of this same Hodge. I recollect him one day scrambling up Dr Johnson's breast, apparently with much satisfaction, while my friend smiling and half-whistling, rubbed down his back, and pulled him by the tail; and when I observed he was a fine cat, saying, 'Why yes, Sir, but I have had cats whom I have liked better than this;' and then as if perceiving Hodge to be out of countenance, adding, 'But he is a very fine cat, a very fine cat indeed.'

From *Life of Johnson*

# CAT

There is a cat that sleeps at night,
That takes delight
In visions bright,
And not a vagrant that creeps at night
On box cars by the river.

This is a sleepy cat to purr
And rarely stir
Its shining fur;
This is a cat whose softest purr
Means salmon, steaks and liver.

This is a cat respectable,
Connectable
With selectable
Feline families respectable,
Whose names would make you quiver.
This is a cat of piety,
Not satiety,
But sobriety,
Its very purr is of piety,
And thanks to its Feline Giver.

And this is how it prays:

'Ancient of Days,
With whiskers torrendous,
Hark to our praise,
Lick and defend us.
Lo, how we bring to Thee
Sweet breasts of mouses,
Hark how we sing to Thee
Filling all houses
With ardent miouses,
Until it arouses
All mankind to battery.
Thou of the golden paws
Thou of the silver claws
Thy tail is the comet's cause,
King of all cattery!'

# The Family Cat

This cat was bought upon the day
That marked the Japanese defeat;
He was anonymous and gay,
But timorous and not discreet.

Although three years have gone, he shows
Fresh sides of his uneven mind:
To us – fond, lenient – he grows
Still more eccentric and refined.

He is a grey, white-chested cat,
And barred with black along the grey;
Not large, and the reverse of fat,
His profile good from either way.

The poet buys especial fish,
Which is made ready by his wife;
The poet's son holds out the dish:
They thus maintain the creature's life.

It's not his anniversary
Alone that's his significance:
In any case mortality
May not be thought of in his presence.

For brief as are our lives, more brief
Exist. Our stroking hides the bones,
Which none the less cry out in grief
Beneath the mocking, loving tones.

# How the Cat Came to Live with Man

*[All Cat really wants to do is lie in a tree and play his violin, but the other animals keep on at him to get a job. So at last he calls on Man.]*

Man was so surprised to see Cat that at first he just stood, eyes wide, mouth open. No creature ever dared to come on to his fields, let alone knock at his door. Cat spoke first.

'I've come for a job,' he said.

'A job?' asked Man, hardly able to believe his ears.

'Work,' said Cat. 'I want to earn my living.'

Man looked him up and down, then saw his long claws.

'You look as if you'd make a fine rat-catcher,' said Man.

Cat was surprised to hear that. He wondered what it was about him that made him look like a rat-catcher. Still, he wasn't going to miss the chance of a job. So he stuck out his chest and said: 'Been doing it for years.'

'Well then, I've a job for you,' said Man. 'My farm's swarming with rats and mice. They're in my haystacks, they're in my cornstacks, and they're all over the pantry.'

So before Cat knew where he was, he had been signed on as a Rat and Mouse Catcher. His pay was milk, and meat, and a place at the fireside. He slept all day and worked all night.

At first he had a terrible time. The rats pulled his tail, the mice nipped his ears. They climbed on to rafters above him and dropped down – thump! on to him in the dark. They teased the life out of him.

But Cat was a quick learner. At the end of the week he could lay out a dozen rats and twice as many mice within half an hour. If he'd gone on laying them out all night there would pretty soon have been none left, and Cat would have been out of a job. So he just caught a few each night – in the first ten minutes or so. Then he retired into the barn and played his violin till morning. This was just the job he had been looking for.

Man was delighted with him. And Mrs Man thought he was beautiful. She took him on her lap and stroked him for hours on end. What a life! thought Cat. If only those silly creatures in the dripping wet woods could see him now!

Well, when the other farmers saw what a fine rat and mouse catcher Cat was, they all wanted cats too. Soon there were so many cats that our Cat decided to form a string band. Oh yes, they were all great violinists. Every night, after making one pile of rats and another of mice, each cat left his farm and was away over the fields to a little dark spinney.

Then what tunes! All night long . . .

Pretty soon lady cats began to arrive. Now, every night, instead of just music, there was dancing too. And what dances! If only you could have crept up there and peeped into the glade from behind a tree and seen the cats dancing – the glossy furred ladies and the tomcats, some pearly grey, some ginger red, and all with wonderful green flashing eyes. Up and down the glade, with the music flying out all over the night.

At dawn they hung their violins in the larch trees, dashed back to the farms, and pretended they had been working all night among the rats and mice. They lapped their milk hungrily, stretched out at the fireside, and fell asleep with smiles on their faces.

From *How the Whale Became and Other Stories*

# Skimbleshanks: the Railway Cat

There's a whisper down the line at 11.39
When the Night Mail's ready to depart,
Saying 'Skimble where is Skimble has he gone to hunt the thimble?
We must find him or the train can't start.'
All the guards and all the porters and the stationmaster's daughters
They are searching high and low,
Saying 'Skimble where is Skimble for unless he's very nimble
Then the Night Mail just can't go.'
At 11.42 then the signal's nearly due
And the passengers are frantic to a man –
Then Skimble will appear and he'll saunter to the rear:
He's been busy in the luggage van!
 He gives one flash of his glass-green eyes
  And the signal goes 'All Clear!'
 And we're off at last for the northern part
  Of the Northern Hemisphere!

You may say that by and large it is Skimble who's in charge
Of the Sleeping Car Express.
From the driver and the guards to the bagmen playing cards
He will supervise them all, more or less.
Down the corridor he paces and examines all the faces
Of the travellers in the First and in the Third;
He establishes control by a regular patrol
And he'd know at once if anything occurred.
He will watch you without winking and he sees what you are thinking
And it's certain that he doesn't approve
Of hilarity and riot, so the folk are very quiet
When Skimble is about and on the move.
 You can play no pranks with Skimbleshanks!
  He's a Cat that cannot be ignored;
 So nothing goes wrong on the Northern Mail
  When Skimbleshanks is aboard.

Oh it's very pleasant when you have found your little den
With your name written up on the door.
And the berth is very neat with a newly folded sheet
And there's not a speck of dust on the floor.
There is every sort of light – you can make it dark or bright;
There's a button that you turn to make a breeze.
There's a funny little basin you're supposed to wash your face in
And a crank to shut the window if you sneeze.
Then the guard looks in politely and will ask you very brightly
'Do you like your morning tea weak or strong?'
But Skimble's just behind him and was ready to remind him,
For Skimble won't let anything go wrong.
    And when you creep into your cosy berth
        And pull up the counterpane,
You are bound to admit that it's very nice
To know that you won't be bothered by mice –
You can leave all that to the Railway Cat,
    The Cat of the Railway Train!

In the middle of the night he is always fresh and bright;
Every now and then he has a cup of tea
With perhaps a drop of Scotch while he's keeping on the watch,
Only stopping here and there to catch a flea.
You were fast asleep at Crewe and so you never knew
That he was walking up and down the station;
You were sleeping all the while he was busy at Carlisle,
Where he greets the stationmaster with elation.
But you saw him at Dumfries, where he summons the police
If there's anything they ought to know about:
When you get to Gallowgate there you do not have to wait –
For Skimbleshanks will help you to get out!
    He gives you a wave of his long brown tail
        Which says: 'I'll see you again!
    You'll meet without fail on the Midnight Mail
        The Cat of the Railway Train.'

# Cat Overboard!

A most tragical Incident fell out this day at Sea. While the Ship was under Sail, but making, as it will appear, no great Way, a Kitten, one of four of the Feline Inhabitants of the Cabin, fell from the Window into Water: an Alarm was immediately given to the Captain, who was then upon Deck, and received it with the utmost Concern. He immediately gave Orders to the Steersman in favour of the poor Thing, as he called it; the Sails were instantly slackened, and all Hands, as the Phrase is, employed to recover the poor Animal. I was, I own, extremely surprised at all this; less, indeed, at the Captain's extreme Tenderness, than at his conceiving any Possibility of Success; for, if Puss had had nine thousand, instead of nine Lives, I concluded they had been all lost. The Boatswain, however, had more sanguine Hopes; for, having stript himself of his Jacket, Breeches, and Shirt, he leapt boldly into the Water, and, to my great Astonishment, in a few Minutes, returned to the Ship, bearing the motionless Animal in his Mouth. Nor was this, I observed, a Matter of such great Difficulty as it appeared to my Ignorance, and possibly may seem to that of my Fresh-water Reader: the Kitten was now exposed to Air and Sun on the Deck, where its Life, of which it retained no Symptoms, was despaired of by all.

The Captain's humanity, if I may so call it, did not so totally destroy his Philosophy, as to make him yield himself up to affliction on this melancholy Occasion. Having felt his Loss like a Man, he resolved to shew he could bear it like one; and, having declared, he had rather have lost a Cask of Rum or Brandy, betook himself to threshing at Backgammon with the *Portuguese* Friar, in which innocent Amusement they passed their leisure hours.

But as I have, perhaps, a little too wantonly endeavoured to raise the tender Passions of my Readers, in this Narrative, I should think myself unpardonable if I concluded it, without giving them the Satisfaction of hearing that the Kitten at last recovered, to the great Joy of the good Captain.

From *Journal of a Voyage to Lisbon*

# Problem

The wind is in the north, the wind
Unfurls its fury at the door;
To turn the cat out seems unkind.

To use him ill I do abhor,
Yet this reflection comes to mind:
Suppose he desecrates the floor?

Though hateful what he'll leave behind,
(To cleanse which were a loathsome chore)
To turn the cat out seems unkind.

He eats a lot, and cries for more:
Roughage, alas, which does not bind:
Suppose he desecrates the floor?

But what if with the dawn I find
Him frozen stiff, and frosted o'er?
To turn the cat out seems unkind.

I'll leave my lino with a score
Of daily journals amply lined:
Suppose he desecrates the floor?
To turn the cat out seems unkind.

## Miss Tibbles

Miss Tibbles is my kitten; white
As day she is and black as night.

She moves in little gusts and breezes
Sharp and sudden as a sneeze is.

At hunting Tibbles has no match,
How I like to see her catch

Moth or beetle, two a penny,
And feast until there isn't any!

Or, if they 'scape her, see her eyes
Grow big as saucers with surprise.

Sometimes I like her calm, unwild,
Gentle as a sleeping child,

And wonder as she lies, a fur ring,
Curled upon my lap, unstirring,
Is it me or Tibbles purring?

# The Naming of Cats

It occurs to me as I write this that the naming of cats is an almost infallible guide to the degree of affection bestowed on a cat. Perhaps not affection so much as true appreciation of feline character. You may be reasonably sure that when you meet a cat called Ginger or Nigger or merely Puss that his or her owner has insufficient respect for his cat. Such plebeian and un-imaginative names are not given to cats by true cat-lovers. There is a world of difference between the commonplace 'Tibby' and the dignified and sonorous 'Tabitha Longclaws Tiddleywinks' which the poet Hood christened his cat. And her three kittens called Pepperpot, Scratchaway and Sootikins reveal an affectionate interest which is never displayed by such ordinary names as Sandy and Micky.

We cannot all rise, of course, to Southey's heights. He, you may remember, called his cat 'the most noble the Archduke Rumpelstiltzchen, Marcus Macbum, Earl Tomlefnagne, Baron Raticide, Waowhler and Scratch'. When summoning His Excellency to a saucer of milk, no doubt 'Rumpel' sufficed, but Southey undoubtedly had the right idea.

Not that grandiloquent or fancy titles are necessary to a true appreci-ation of cats. What could be more dignified or appropriate than the name of Dr Johnson's cat Hodge? . . .

Without doubt the names given to individual cats shed interesting light on their human owners. No one but a true cat lover could call his cat Gilderoy, Absolom, Potiphar, Wotan, Feathers or Shah de Perse.

It may be thought that such elegant names are difficult to live up to, and it is true that in ordinary usage even the most fervent cat-lover will use a convenient abbreviation. But I am sure every true lover of cats will agree that there are times when nothing less than full ceremonial titles will serve.

From *Charles, the Story of a Friendship*

# The Owl and the Pussy-Cat

The Owl and the Pussy-Cat went to sea
   In a beautiful pea-green boat,
They took some honey, and plenty of money,
   Wrapped up in a five-pound note.
The Owl looked up to the stars above,
   And sang to a small guitar,
'O lovely Pussy! O Pussy, my love,
   What a beautiful Pussy you are,
     You are,
     You are!
   What a beautiful Pussy you are!

Pussy said to the Owl, 'You elegant fowl!
   How charmingly sweet you sing!
O let us be married! too long we have tarried
   But what shall we do for a ring?
They sailed away for a year and a day,
   To the land where the Bong-tree grows,
And there in a wood a Piggy-wig stood,
   With a ring at the end of his nose,
     His nose,
     His nose,
   With a ring at the end of his nose.

'Dear Pig, are you willing to sell for one shilling
   Your ring?' Said the Piggy, 'I will.'
So they took it away, and were married next day
   By the Turkey who lives on the hill.
They dined on mince, and slices of quince,
   Which they ate with a runcible spoon;
And hand in hand, on the edge of the sand,
   They danced by the light of the moon,
     The moon,
     The moon,
   They danced by the light of the moon.

# Montmorency Thinks He Will Murder an Old Tom Cat

We were, as I have said, returning from a dip, and half-way up the High Street when a cat darted out from one of the houses in front of us, and began to trot across the road. Montmorency gave a cry of joy – the cry of a stern warrior who sees his enemy given over to his hands – the sort of cry Cromwell might have uttered when the Scots came down the hill – and flew after his prey.

His victim was a large black Tom. I never saw a larger cat, nor a more disreputable-looking cat. It had lost half its tail, one of its ears, and a fairly appreciable proportion of its nose. It was a long, sinewy-looking animal. It had a calm, contented air about it.

Montmorency went for that poor cat at the rate of twenty miles an hour; but the cat did not hurry up – did not seem to have grasped the idea that its life was in danger. It trotted quietly on until its would-be assassin was within a yard of it, and then it turned round and sat down in the middle of the road, and looked at Montmorency with a gentle, inquiring expression, that said:

'Yes! You want me?'

Montmorency does not lack pluck; but there was something about the look of that cat that might have chilled the heart of the boldest dog. He stopped abruptly, and looked back at Tom.

Neither spoke; but the conversation that one could imagine was clearly as follows:

THE CAT: Can I do anything for you?

MONTMORENCY: No – no thanks.

THE CAT: Don't mind speaking, if you really want anything, you know.

MONTMORENCY *(backing down the High Street)*: Oh, no – not at all – certainly – don't you trouble. I – I'm afraid I've made a mistake. I thought I knew you. Sorry I disturbed you.

THE CAT: Not at all – quite a pleasure. Sure you don't want anything, now?

MONTMORENCY *(still backing)*: Not at all, thanks – not at all – very kind of you. Good morning.

THE CAT: Good morning.

Then the cat rose, and continued his trot; and Montmorency, fitting what he calls his tail carefully into its groove, came back to us, and took up an unimportant position in the rear.

To this day, if you say the word 'Cats!' to Montmorency, he will visibly shrink and look up piteously at you, as if to say:

'Please don't!'                          From *Three Men in a Boat*

# Garden-Lion

O Michael, you are at once the enemy
And the chief ornament of our garden,
Scrambling up rose-posts, nibbling at nepeta,
Making your lair where tender plants should flourish,
Or proudly couchant on a sun-warmed stone.

What do you do all night there, When we seek our soft beds,
And you go off, old roisterer,
Away into the dark?

I think you play at leopards and panthers;
I think you wander on to foreign properties;
But on winter mornings you are a lost orphan
Pitifully wailing underneath our windows;

And in summer, by the open doorway,
You come in pad, pad, lazily to breakfast,
Plumy tail waving, with a fine swagger,
Like a drum-major, or a parish beadle,
Or a rich rajah, or the Grand Mogul.

# War Cat

I am sorry, my little cat, I am sorry –
If I had it, you should have it;
but there's a war on.

No, there are no table scraps;
there was only an omelette
made from dehydrated eggs,
and baked apples to follow,
and we finished it all.
The butcher has no lights,
the fishmonger has no cods' heads –
there is nothing for you
but cat-biscuit
and those remnants of yesterday's ham;
you must do your best with it.

Round and pathetic eyes,
baby mouth opened in a reproachful cry,
how can I explain to you?
I know, I know –
'Mistress, it is not nice;
the ham is very salt
and the cat-biscuit very dull,
I sniffed at it, and the smell was not enticing.
Do you not love me any more?
Mistress, I do my best for the war-effort;
I killed four mice last week,
Yesterday I caught a young stoat,
you stroked me and praised me,
you called me a clever cat.
What have I done to offend you?
I am industrious, I earn my keep;
I am not like the parrot, who sits there
using bad language and devouring
parrot-seed at eight-and-sixpence a pound
without working for it.
If you will not pay me my wages
there is no justice;
if you have ceased to love me
there is no charity.

See now, I rub myself against your legs
to express my devotion,
which is not altered by any unkindness.
My little heart is contracted
because your goodwill is withdrawn from me;
my ribs are rubbing together
for lack of food,
but indeed I cannot eat this –
my soul revolts at the sight of it.
I have tried, believe me,
but it was like ashes in my mouth.
If your favour is departed
and your bowls of compassion are shut up,
then all that is left of me
is to sit in a draught on the stone floor and look miserable
till I die of starvation
and a broken heart.'

Cat with the innocent face
what can I say?
Everything is very hard on everybody.
If you were a little Greek cat,
or a little Polish cat,
there would be nothing for you at all,
not even Cat-Food:
indeed you would be lucky
if you were not eaten yourself.
Think if you were a little Russian cat
prowling among the condors of a deserted city!
Consider that pains and labour,
and the valour of merchant-seamen and fishermen
have gone even to the making of this biscuit
which smells so unappetising.
Alas! there is no language
in which I can tell you of these things.

Well, well!
if you will not be comforted
we will put the contents of your saucer
into the chicken-bowl – there!
all gone! nasty old cat-food –
the hens, I dare say,
will be grateful for it.

Wait only a little
and I will go to the butcher
and see if by any chance
he can produce some fragments of the insides of something.
Only stop crying
and staring in that unbearable manner –
as soon as I have put on my hat
we will try to do something about it.

My hat is on,
I have put on my shoes,
I have taken my shopping-basket –
What are you doing on the table?

The chicken-bowl is licked clean;
there is nothing left in it at all.
Cat,
Hell-cat, Hitler-cat, human,
all-too-human cat,
cat corrupt, infected,
instinct with original sin,
cat of a fallen and perverse creation,
hypocrite with the innocent and limpid eyes –
is nothing desirable
till somebody else desires it?
is anything and everything attractive
so long as it is got by stealing?
Furtive and squalid cat,
green glance, squinted over a cringing shoulder,
streaking hurriedly out the back door
in expectation of judgement,
your manners and morals are perfectly abhorrent to me,
you dirty little thief and liar.

Nevertheless,
although you have made a fool of me,
yet, bearing in mind your pretty wheedling ways,
(not to mention the four mice and the immature stoat),
and having put my hat on to go to the butcher's,
I may as well go.

# *From* The Cat that Knew Hell

[*An alley cat from the Rue de Lambre in Paris is given a comfortable home.*]

. . . The one-time blade of a cat became dull and cumbersome of movement; his wicked gnome-slit amber eyes were glazed with oversleep. His sides bulged with gorged chicken and lapped milk. He was to all intents and purposes a nice cat . . .

But there are times when into the cat's lethargic cream-bemuddled brain creeps a wistful memory of the glory that is past. It is mostly at dusk that this memory comes, when the neat capped and aproned maid enters the salon to draw the heavy chenille curtains across the long French windows, and for one instant the street lights blaze out through the night mist before they are shut out from view by red chenille. It is then that the cat remembers the Rue de Lambre. He sees once again the stalls, hears the high-pitched voices of the stall-holders raised in strident fury against him, sees the little spurting flames of Hell, and feels his claws lengthening, his muscles growing taut, and the wild madcap call to murderous action surging through his blood.

Ah, the intoxication of scattering Madame Tiron's cabbages to the four winds! The joy of digging deep in Madame Bouchier's snail barrel! The delight of seeing the girl from the *boulangerie* sprawling upon the *trottoir* on top of her basket of *petits pains!* The fiendish anticipation of teeth in white flesh, of claws deep in thick wool or flimsy cotton! Ah, the glory of those past hours when the yellow goblin lights danced in the mist-veiled darkness, when it was spit, scratch, swear, out with everything, down with everyone and long live the devil!

And the cat, with his soft paws padding down his bed on the most delicate and extravagant of all the satin *pouffes*, for yet more slumber, thinks, as sometimes humans think who have repented of their sins and are now on the side of the haloed angels, that after all Hell had its points.

# Mister the Blitzkit

*(For K)*

Double, double, toil and trouble,
Crumps and bumps and lumps of rubble.
Little Mister, six weeks old,
Hungry, dirty, frightened, cold,
Has no mother, home, nor dinner,
But he's sharp for a beginner.
From his crevice he surveys
Those who walk the ruined ways;
From their faces he can tell
Who would treat a kitten well.
The big policeman, good but gruff –
Let him pass; he's rather rough,
And as a conscientious man
Might pop him in a certain Van.
A kindly matron comes to view.
She's nice – but what about the stew?
When her four fat kids have done
There's not much left for anyone.
Besides, those kids would give him hell.
Let her go, then. Wait a spell.
Here's warden; that's a frost –
He's got no home except his post.
Soldier, sailor – damn, no good.
Cripes, he could down a bit of food.
And O hell, here comes the rain.
Stick it, Mister, try again.

Ah, here she comes, the very one!
The fact is obvious as the sun.
Young as he is, now Mister knows
He can bid farewell to woes.
In her countenance he reads
That she will satisfy his needs.
Food, fire, bed – he ticks them off –
Worm-dose, mixture for his cough,
Velvet mouse for when he plays,
Brush and comb, and holidays
In the countryside afar,

Or boarded out with loving char.
She will pick him up correctly
And always touch him circumspectly,
Like a really first-class mother
Never neglect, yet never bother.
The greatest wonder is that he
Knows that there is a vacancy,
Which has allowed a thieving band
Of mice to get the upper hand.

Forth he darts – with piteous grace
Looks up mewing in her face.
Six weeks old – but what a grip
On the art of salesmanship!
Youth, dirt, fear, all play their part
In the lady's feeling heart.
A word of love, a mutual kiss,
And he is hers, and she is his.
Because he is so small and weak
She holds him closely to her cheek,
Takes him home, through wind and rain,
And will not let him go again.

Arrived, he finds he did not err
In his estimate of her.
Warm milk, a nice old woollen vest,
And he soon sinks to blissful rest
When he awakes, his coat will be
Brushed into strict propriety,
And in the evening she will seal
Their love with a substantial meal,
And let him lay his clever head
Close to her own warm heart, in bed.

# The Superiority of Adolphus

For the study of majestic dignity, tinged on occasions with lofty disdain, interpreters of muscular expression would do well to seek out Adolphus. He walks the highway without haste or concern for his personal survival in the midst of tooting automobiles and charging dogs. When a strange dog appears and mistakes Adolphus for an ordinary cat who may be chased for the sport of the thing, it is the custom of Adolphus to slow his pace somewhat and stretch out in the path of the oncoming enemy, assuming the pose and the expression of the sphinx. He is the graven image of repose and perfect muscular control. Only his slumbrous amber eyes burn unblinkingly, never leaving the enraged countenance of his enemy, who bears down on him with exposed fangs and hackles erect. When the assault is too ferocious to be in good taste even among dogs, accompanied by hysterical yapping and snapping, Adolphus has been known to yawn in the face of his assailant, quite deliberately and very politely, as a gentleman of good breeding might when bored by an excessive display of emotion. Usually the dog mysteriously halts within a foot or so of those calm yellow eyes and describes a semi-circle within the range of those twin fires, filling the air with defiant taunts that gradually die away to foolish whimpering as he begins an undignified withdrawal, while Adolphus winks solemnly and stares past his cowering foe into a mysterious space undesecrated by blustering dogs.

A few dogs there have been who have failed to halt at the hypnotic command of those yellow eyes. Then there came a lightning-like flash of fur through the air, and Adolphus landed neatly on his victim's neck, his great claws beginning to rip with businesslike precision through the soft ears and forehead of the terrified dog. Perhaps the rumour of these encounters spread among the canine population of our neighbourhood, for it is never counted against the reputation of any dog as a fighter if he makes a wide detour of the regions frequented by Adolphus . . .

From *The Undoing of Morning Glory Adolphus*

# Cat's Meat

Ho, all you cats in all the street;
Look out, it is the hour of meat;

The little barrow is crawling along,
And the meat-boy growling his fleshy song.

Hurry, Ginger! Hurry, White!
Don't delay to court or fight.

Wandering Tabby, vagrant Black,
Yamble from adventure back!

Slip across the shining street,
Meat! Meat! Meat! Meat!

Lift your tail and dip your feet;
Find your penny – Meat! Meat!

Where's your mistress? Learn to purr:
Pennies emanate from her.

Be to her, for she is Fate,
Perfectly affectionate.

(You, domestic Pinkie-Nose,
Keep inside and warm your toes.)

Flurry, flurry in the street –
Meat! Meat! Meat! Meat!

## Correspondence Between Donald Martin, (Bank Manager), and the Editor

92 Wodeland Avenue,
Guildford.
28 December 1971

Dear Sir,

I understand that you have now commenced a 'Rent-a-Cat' service from your home.

We are interested in your elder cat, Mr Floyd, and shall be glad to be sent your inclusive weekly rental – food to be supplied by your goodselves.

Are your cats sent out on approval or return please?

Yours faithfully,
Donald Martin

RENT-A-CAT LTD
*Proprietor: K. Lillington, Gent.*

29 December 1971

Dear Sir,

We shall be pleased to send you our charges for hiring our cat Floyd, provided that you will assure us that while in your care he will receive proper religious instruction and will not be made to perform menial tasks.

With regard to food, we regret that we are no longer in a position to supply this our goodselves. You will appreciate that with rising costs it is no longer possible to provide the seven heavy meals a day that this animal needs.

Regarding your last question, we generally send our cats to live on other people with the utmost approval.

Yrs etc.,
K. Lillington

# DOUGLAS STEWART

## *From* Lady Feeding the Cats

Shuffling along in her broken shoes from the slums,
A blue-eyed lady showing the weather's stain,
Her long dress green and black like a pine in the rain,
Her bonnet much bedraggled, daily she comes
Uphill past the Moreton Bays and the smoky gums
With a sack of bones on her back and a song in her brain
To feed those outlaws prowling about the Domain,
Those furtive she-cats and those villainous toms.

Proudly they step to meet her, they march together
With an arching of backs and a waving of plumy tails
And smiles; they swear they never would harm a feather.
They rub at her legs for the bounty that never fails,
   They think she is a princess out of a tower,
   And so she is, she is trembling with love and power.

# The Intelligence of Calvin

The intelligence of Calvin was something phenomenal, in his rank of life. He established a method of communicating his wants, and even some of his sentiments; and he could help himself in many things. There was a furnace register in a retired room, where he used to go when he wished to be alone, that he always opened when he desired more heat; but never shut it, any more than he shut the door after himself. He could do almost anything but speak; and you would declare sometimes that you could see a pathetic longing to do that in his intelligent face. I have no desire to overdraw his qualities, but if there was one thing in him more noticeable than another, it was his fondness for nature. He could content himself for hours at a low window, looking into the ravine and at the great trees, noting the smallest stir there; he delighted, above all things, to accompany me walking about the garden, hearing the birds, getting the smell of the fresh earth, and rejoicing in the sunshine. He followed me and gambolled like a dog, rolling over on the turf and exhibiting his delight in a hundred ways. If I worked, he sat and watched me, or looked off over the bank, and kept his ear open to the twitter in the cherry-trees. When it stormed, he was sure to sit at the window, keenly watching the rain or the snow, glancing up and down at its falling; and a winter tempest always delighted him. I think he was genuinely fond of birds, but, so far as I know, he usually confined himself to one a day; he never killed, as some sportsmen do, for the love of killing, but only as civilised people do – from necessity. He was intimate with the flying-squirrels who dwelt in the chestnut-trees – too intimate, for almost every day in the summer he would bring in one, until he nearly discouraged them. He was, indeed, a superb hunter, and would have been a devastating one, if his bump of destructiveness had not been offset by a bump of moderation. There was very little of the brutality of the lower animals about him; I don't think he enjoyed rats for themselves, but he knew his business, and for the first few months of his residence with us he waged an awful campaign against the horde, and after that his simple presence was sufficient to deter them from coming on the premises. Mice amused him, but he usually considered them too small game to be taken seriously; I have seen him play for an hour with a mouse, and then let him go with a royal condescension. In this whole matter of 'getting a living', Calvin was a contrast to the rapacity of the age in which he lived.

From *Calvin, the Cat*

# Milk for the Cat

When the tea is brought at five o'clock,
And all the neat curtains are drawn with care,
The little black cat with bright green eyes
Is suddenly purring there.

At first she pretends, having nothing to do,
She has come in merely to blink by the grate,
But, though tea may be late or the milk may be sour,
She is never late.

And presently her agate eyes
Take a soft large milky haze,
And her independent casual glance
Becomes a stiff, hard gaze.

Then she stamps her claws or lifts her ears,
Or twists her tail and begins to stir,
Till suddenly all her lithe body becomes
One breathing, trembling purr.

The children eat and wriggle and laugh;
The two old ladies stroke their silk:
But the cat is grown small and thin with desire,
Transformed to a creeping lust for milk.

The white saucer like some full moon descends
At last from the clouds of the table above;
She sighs and dreams and thrills and glows,
Transfigured with love.

She nestles over the shining rim,
Buries her chin in the creamy sea;
Her tail hangs loose; each drowsy paw
Is doubled under each bended knee.

A long, dim ecstasy holds her life;
Her world is an infinite shapeless white,
Till her tongue has curled the last holy drop,
Then she sinks back into the night.

Draws and dips her body to heap
Her sleepy nerves in the great armchair,
Lies defeated and buried deep
Three or four hours unconscious there.

# The Singing Cat

It was a little captive cat
   Upon a crowded train
His mistress takes him from his box
   To ease his fretful pain

She holds him tight upon her knee
   The graceful animal
And all the people look at him
   He is so beautiful

But oh he pricks and oh he prods
   And turns upon her knee
Then lifteth up his innocent voice
   In plaintive melody

He lifteth up his innocent voice
   He lifteth up, he singeth
And to each human countenance
   A smile of grace he bringeth

He lifteth up his innocent paw
   Upon her breast he clingeth
And everybody cries, Behold
   The cat, the cat that singeth

He lifteth up his innocent voice
   He lifteth up, he singeth
And all the people warm themselves
   In the love his beauty bringeth

## *From* **The Long Cat**

A short-haired black cat always looks longer than any other cat. But this particular one, Babou, nicknamed the Long-cat, really did measure, stretched right out flat, well over a yard. I used to measure him sometimes.

'He's stopped growing longer,' I said one day to my mother. 'Isn't it a pity?'

'Why a pity? He's too long as it is. I can't understand why you want everything to grow bigger. It's bad to grow too much, very bad indeed.'

It's true that it always worried her when she thought her children were growing too fast, and she had good cause to be anxious about my elder half-brother, who went on growing until he was twenty-four.

'But I'd love to grow a bit taller.'

'D'you mean you'd like to be like that Brisedoux girl, five-feet-seven tall at twelve years old? A midget can always make herself liked. But what can you do with a gigantic beauty? Who would want to marry her?'

'Couldn't Babou get married then?'

'Oh, a cat's a cat. Babou's only too long when he really wants to be. Are we even sure he's black? He's probably white in snowy weather, dark blue at night, and red when he goes to steal strawberries. He's very light when he lies on your knees, and very heavy when I carry him into the kitchen in the evenings to prevent him from sleeping on my bed. I think he's too much of a vegetarian to be a real cat.'

For the Long-cat really did steal strawberries, picking out the ripest of the variety called Docteur-Morere which are so sweet, and of the Haut-boys which taste faintly of nuts. According to the season he would also go for the tender tips of the asparagus, and when it came to melons his choice was not so much for cantaloups as for the kind called Noir-des-Carmes whose rind, marbled light and dark like the skin of a salamander, he knew how to rip open. In all this he was not exceptional. I once had a she-cat who used to crunch rings of raw onion, provided they were the sweet onions of the South. There are cats who set great store by oysters, snails, and clams . . .

By virtue of his serpent-like build, the Long-cat excelled in strange leaps in which he nearly twisted himself into a figure of eight. In full sunlight his winter coat, which was longer and more satiny than in summer, revealed the waterings and markings of his far-off tabby ances-tor. A tom will remain playful until he is quite old; but even in play his face never loses the gravity that is stamped on it. The Long-cat's expression softened only when he looked at my mother. Then his white whiskers would bristle powerfully, while into his eyes crept the smile of an innocent little boy. He used to follow her when she went to pick violets along the wall that separated M. de Fourolles' garden from ours. The close-set border provided every day a big bunch which mother let fade, either pinned to her bodice or in an empty glass, because violets in water lose all their scent. Step by step the Long-cat followed his stooping mistress, sometimes imitating with his paw the gesture of her hand groping among the leaves, and imitating her discoveries also. 'Ha, ha!' he would cry, 'me too!' and thereupon show his prize: a bombardier beetle, a pink worm, or a shrivelled cockchafer.

*Translated from the French by Enid McLeod*

# My Cat Jeoffry

For I will consider my cat Jeoffry.

For he is the servant of the Living God, duly and daily serving Him.

For at first glance of the Glory of God in the East he worships in his way.

For is this done by wreathing his body seven times round with elegant quickness.

For then he leaps up to catch the musk, which is the blessing of God on his prayer.

For he rolls upon prank to work it in.

For having done duty, and received blessing, he begins to consider himself.

For this he performs in ten degrees.

For first he looks upon his forepaws to see if they are clean.

For secondly he kicks up behind to clear away there.

For thirdly he works it upon stretch with the forepaws extended.

For fourthly he sharpens his paws by wood.

For fifthly he washes himself.

For sixthly he rolls upon wash.

For seventhly he fleas himself, that he may not be interrupted upon the beat.

For eighthly he rubs himself against a post.

For ninthly he looks up for his instructions.

For tenthly he goes in quest of food.

For having considered God and himself he will consider his neighbour.

For if he meets another cat he will kiss her in kindness.

For when he takes his prey he plays with it to give it a chance.

For one mouse in seven escapes by his dallying.

For when his day's work is done his business more properly begins.

For he keeps the Lord's watch in the night against the Adversary.

For he counteracts the Devil, who is death, by brisking about the life.

For in his morning orisons he loves the sun and the sun loves him.

For he is of the tribe of Tiger.

For the Cherub Cat is a term of the Angel Tiger.

For he has the subtlety and hiss of the serpent, which in goodness he suppresses.

For he will not do destruction, if he is well-fed, neither will he spit without provocation.

For he purrs in thankfulness, when God tells him he's a good Cat.

For he is an instrument for the children to learn benevolence upon.

For every house is incomplete without him and a blessing is lacking in the spirit.

For the Lord commanded Moses concerning the cats at the departure of the Children of Israel from Egypt.

For every family had one cat at least in the bag.

For the English cats are the best in Europe.

For he is the cleanest in the use of his forepaws of any quadrupede.

For the dexterity of his defence is an instance of the love of God to him exceedingly.

For he is the quickest to his mark of any creature.

For he is tenacious of his point.

For he is a mixture of gravity and waggery.

For he knows that God is his Saviour.

For there is nothing sweeter than his peace when at rest.

For there is nothing brisker than his life when in motion.

For he is of the Lord's poor and so indeed is he called by benevolence perpetually – Poor Jeoffry! poor Jeoffry! the rat has bit thy throat.

For I bless the name of the Lord Jesus that Jeoffry is better.

For the divine spirit comes about his body to sustain it in complete cat.

For his tongue is exceeding pure so that it has in purity what it wants in music.

For he is docile and can learn certain things.

For he can set up with gravity which is patience upon approbation.

For he can fetch and carry, which is patience in employment.

For he can jump over a stick which is patience upon proof positive.

For he can spraggle upon waggle at the word of command.

For he can jump from an eminence into his master's bosom.

For he can catch the cork and toss it again.

For he is hated by the hypocrite and miser.

For the former is afraid of detection.

And the latter refuses the charge.

For he camels his back to bear the first notion of business.

For he is good to think on, if a man would express himself neatly.

For he made a great figure in Egypt for his signal services.

For he killed the Ichneumon-rat very pernicious by land.

For his ears are so acute that they sting again.

For from this proceeds the passing quickness of his attention.

For by stroking of him I have found out electricity.

For I perceive God's light about him both wax and fire.

For the electrical fire is the spiritual substance, which God sends from heaven to sustain the bodies of both man and beast.

For God has blessed him in the variety of his movements.

For, tho he cannot fly, he is an excellent clamberer.

For his motions upon the face of the earth are more than any other quadrupede.

For he can tread to all the measures upon the music.
For he can swim for life.
For he can creep.

# For Worse

Seven of the twelve cats in this section are dead, including one by drowning and one by hanging, so, if life is a boon, we can call them unlucky. R. M. Ballantyne's cat who has the Curious Conversation with Peterkin is thrown into the sea by his tail by pirates a few pages later. Of the other four, Emily Dickinson's and William Cowper's cats are discomfited, E. V. Rieu's cat is missing, and C. S. Calverley's cat has seen better days. One or two of the obituary poems are so sad that it's unfair.

# THOMAS GRAY

## On a Favourite Cat Drowned in a Tub of Goldfishes

'Twas on a lofty vase's side,
Where China's gayest art had dy'd
   The azure flowers that blow;
Demurest of the tabby kind,
The pensive Selima reclin'd,
   Gaz'd on the lake below.

Her conscious tail her joy declar'd;
The fair round face, the snowy beard,
   The velvet of her paws,
Her coat, that with the tortoise vies,
Her ears of jet, and emerald eyes,
   She saw; and purr'd applause.

Still had she gaz'd, but 'midst the tide
Two angel forms were seen to glide,
   The Genii of the stream:
Their scaly armour's Tyrian hue
Thro' richest purple to the view
   Betray'd a golden gleam.

The hapless Nymph with wonder saw:
A whisker first and then a claw,
   With many an ardent wish,
She stretch'd in vain to reach the prize.
What female heart can gold despise?
   What Cat's averse to fish?

Presumptuous maid! with looks intent
Again she stretch'd, again she bent,
   Nor knew the gulf between.
(Malignant Fate sat by, and smil'd)
The slipp'ry verge her feet beguiled;
   She tumbled headlong in.

Eight times emerging from the flood
She mew'd to ev'ry watery god
   Some speedy aid to send.
No Dolphin came, no Neruid stirr'd,
Nor cruel *Tom* nor *Susan* heard.
   A fav'rite has no friend!

From hence, ye Beauties, undeceiv'd,
Know one false step is ne'er retriev'd,
   And be with caution bold.
Not all that tempts your wand'ring eyes
And heedless hearts, is lawful prize;
   Nor all that glisters, gold.

# Cat

She sights a Bird – she chuckles –
She flattens – then she crawls –
She runs without the look of feet –
Her eyes increase to Balls –

Her jaws stir – twitching – hungry –
Her Teeth can hardly stand –
She leaps, but Robin leaped the first –
Ah, Pussy, of the Sand.

The Hopes so juicy ripening –
You almost bathed your Tongue –
When Bliss disclosed a hundred Toes –
And fled with every one –

# Death of the Cat

Alas! Mowler, the children's pride,
Has slipped on a water-butt, tumbled inside
And died.

The seamstress on her sewing machine
Stitched a shroud of satin sheen.

The carpenter hammered and planed a coffin
Of seasoned oak without a knot in.

The sexton – he loved dear Mowler well –
Mournfully, mournfully tolled the bell.

Few were the prayers the parson spoke.
All he could do, poor fellow, was choke.

But saddest of all in the funeral train
Were the children. Deep were their sorrow and pain.

For they knew, as they followed the churchyard through,
They'd never set eyes on Mowler again.

In silence behind the coffin they stepped,
Solemnly, slowly. Everyone wept.

Except
The little mice hid in the hedge – not they!
'Twas not *their* hearts that bled.
'Let's out and play,'
They cried. 'Oh, spread
The butter thick on the bread!
Dance in cream cheese right up to our knees,
For the cat is dead!
Hooray!
The cat
     is
        dead!'

# The Lost Cat

She took a last and simple meal when there were none to see her steal –
    A jug of cream upon the shelf, a fish prepared for dinner;
And now she walks a distant street with delicately sandalled feet,
    And no one gives her much to eat or weeps to see her thinner.

O my beloved come again, come back in joy, come back in pain,
    To end our searching with a mew, or with a purr our grieving;
And you shall have for lunch or tea whatever fish swim in the sea
    And all the cream that's meant for me – and not a word of thieving!

# Cat's Funeral

    Bury her deep, down deep,
    Safe in the earth's cold keep,
    Bury her deep –

    No more to watch bird stir;
    No more to clean dark fur;
No more to glisten as silk;
No more to revel in milk;
    No more to purr.

    Bury her deep, down deep;
    She is beyond warm sleep.
She will not walk in the night;
She will not wake to the light.
    Bury her deep.

# WILLIAM COWPER

## The Retired Cat

A poet's cat, sedate and grave,
As poet well could wish to have,
Was much addicted to enquire
For nooks, to which she might retire,
And where, secure as mouse in chink,
She might repose, or sit and think.
I know not where she caught the trick –
Nature perhaps herself had cast her
In such a mould PHILOSOPHIQUE,
Or else she learned it of her master.
Sometimes ascending, debonair,
An apple-tree or lofty pear,
Lodg'd with convenience in the fork,
She watch'd the gard'ner at his work;
Sometimes her ease and solace sought
In an old empty wat'ring pot,
There wanting nothing, save a fan,
To seem some nymph in her sedan,
Apparell'd in exactest sort,
And ready to be borne to court.
  But love of change it seems has place
Not only in our wiser race;
Cats also feel as well as we
That passions's force, and so did she.
Her climbing, she began to find,
Expos'd her too much to the wind,
And the old utensil of tin
Was cold and comfortless within:
She therefore wish'd instead of those,
Some place of more serene repose,
Where neither cold might come, nor air
Too rudely wanton with her hair,
And sought it in the likeliest mode
Within her master's snug abode.
  A draw'r, – it chanc'd, at bottom lin'd
With linen of the softest kind,
With such as merchants introduce
From India, for the ladies' use, –
A draw'r impending o'er the rest,
Half open in the topmost chest,

Of depth enough, and none to spare,
Invited her to slumber there.
Puss with delight beyond expression,
Surveyed the scene, and took possession.
Recumbent at her ease ere long,
And lull'd by her own hum-drum song,
She left the cares of life behind,
And slept as she would sleep her last,
When in came, housewifely inclin'd,
The chambermaid, and shut it fast,
By no malignity impell'd,
But all unconscious whom it held.

   Awaken'd by the shock (cried puss)
Was ever cat attended thus!
The open draw'r was left, I see,
Merely to make a nest for me,
For soon as I was well compos'd,
There came the maid, and it was clos'd:
How smooth these kerchiefs, and how sweet,
O what a delicate retreat!
I will resign myself to rest
Till Sol, declining in the west,
Shall call to supper; when, no doubt,
Susan will come and let me out.

   The evening came, the sun descended,
And puss remain'd still unattended.
The night roll'd tardily away,
(With her indeed 'twas never day)
The sprightly morn her course renew'd,
The evening gray again ensued,
And puss came into mind no more
Than if entomb'd the day before.
With hunger pinch'd, and pinch'd for room,
She now presag'd approaching doom,
Nor slept a single wink, or purr'd,
Conscious of jeopardy incurr'd.

   That night, by chance, the poet watching,
Heard an inexplicable scratching,
His noble heart went pit-a-pat,
And to himself he said – what's that?
He drew the curtain at his side,
And forth he peep'd, but nothing spied.
Yet, by his ear directed, guess'd

Something imprison'd in the chest,
And doubtful what, with prudent care,
Resolv'd it should continue there.
At length a voice, which well he knew,
A long and melancholy mew,
Saluting his poetic ears,
Consol'd him, and dispell'd his fears;
He left his bed, he trod the floor,
He 'gan in haste the draw'rs explore,
The lowest first, and without stop,
The rest in order to the top.
For 'tis a truth well known to most,
That whatsoever thing is lost,
We seek it, ere it come to light,
In ev'ry cranny but the right.
Forth skipp'd the cat; not now replete
As erst with airy self-conceit,
Nor in her own fond apprehension,
A theme for all the world's attention,
But modest, sober, cur'd of all
Her notions hyperbolical,
'And wishing for a place of rest
Any thing rather than a chest:
Then stept the poet into bed,
With this reflexion in his head:

MORAL

Beware of too sublime a sense
Of your own worth and consequence!
The man who dreams himself so great,
And his importance of such weight,
That all around, in all that's done,
Must move and act for him alone,
Will learn, in school of tribulation,
The folly of his expectation.

# Cat Dying in Autumn

I put the cat outside to die,
Laying her down
Into a rut of leaves
Cold and bloodsoaked;
Her moan
Coming now more quiet
And brief in October's economy
Till the jaws
Opened and shut on no sound.

Behind the wide pane
I watched the dying cat
Whose fur like a veil of air
The autumn wind stirred
Indifferently with the leaves;
Her form (or was it the wind?)
Still breathing –
A surprise of white.

And I was thinking
Of melting snow in spring
Or a strip of gauze
When a sparrow
Dropped down beside it
Leaning his clean beak
Into the hollow;
Then whirred away, his wings,
You may suppose, shuddering.

Letting me see
From my house
The twisted petal
That fell
Between the ruined paws
To hold or play with,
And the tight smile
Cats have for meeting death.

# R. M. BALLANTYNE

## A Curious Conversation with a Cat

The sight that met our gaze was certainly not a little amusing. On the top of a log which we sometimes used as a table, sat the black cat, with a very demure expression on its countenance; and in front of it, sitting on the ground, with his legs extended on either side of the log, was Peterkin. At the moment we saw him he was gazing intently into the cat's face, with his nose about four inches from it – his hand being thrust into his breeches pocket.

'Cat,' said Peterkin, turning his head a little on one side, 'I love you!'

There was a pause, as if Peterkin awaited a reply to his affectionate declaration. But the cat said nothing.

'Do you hear me?' cried Peterkin, sharply. 'I love you – I do. Don't you love me?'

To this touching appeal the cat said 'Mew,' faintly.

'Ah! that's right. You're a jolly old rascal. Why did you not speak at once, eh?' and Peterkin put forward his mouth and kissed the cat on the nose!

'Yes,' continued Peterkin, after a pause, 'I love you. D'you think I'd say so if I didn't, you black villain? I love you because I've got to take care of you, and to look after you, and to think about you, and to see that you don't die – '

'Mew, me-a-aw!' said the cat.

'Very good,' continued Peterkin, 'quite true, I have no doubt; but you've no right to interrupt me, sir. Hold your tongue till I have done speaking. Moreover, cat, I love you because you came to me the first time you ever saw me, and didn't seem to be afraid, and appeared to be fond of me, though you didn't know that I wasn't going to kill you. Now, that was brave, that was bold, and very jolly, old boy, and I love you for it – I do!'

Again there was a pause of a few minutes, during which the cat looked placid, and Peterkin dropped his eyes upon its toes as if in contemplation. Suddenly he looked up.

'Well, cat, what are you thinking about now? Won't speak, eh? Now, tell me; don't you think it's a monstrous shame that these two scoundrels, Ralph and Jack, should keep us waiting for our supper so long?'

Here the cat arose, put up its back and stretched itself; yawned slightly, and licked the point of Peterkin's nose!

'Just so, old boy, you're a clever fellow – I really do believe the brute understands me!' said Peterkin, while a broad grin overspread his face, as he drew back and surveyed the cat.

At this point Jack burst into a loud fit of laughter. The cat uttered an angry fuff and fled, while Peterkin sprang up and exclaimed:

63

'Bad luck to you, Jack! you've nearly made the heart jump out of my body, you have!'

'Perhaps I have,' replied Jack, laughing, as we entered the bower, 'But, as I don't intend to keep you or the cat any longer from our supper, I hope that you'll both forgive me.'

Peterkin endeavoured to turn this affair off with a laugh, but I observed that he blushed very deeply at the time we discovered ourselves, and he did not seem to relish any allusion to the subject afterwards; so we refrained from remarking on it ever after – though it tickled us not a little at the time.

From *The Coral Island*

# Death of a Cat

Always fastidious, it removed its dying
From us, and lay down by it in the dark
As if death were a mouse, and a cat's role
To deal with it, and not involve the house;
Chose a remote spot that, when I bent to help,
Shocked because it existed – I had thought
The mind a complete map of home; left dust
On my fingers when I had settled it
In front of the fire on an old blanket;
Insisted to the last on standing
And walking with frail dignity to its water
In its usual place in the kitchen, disdaining
The saucer we had thoughtfully set near it.

And death was a wind that tested regularly
The strength the cat had left, and in its walk
Puffed on its flank and made it totter
Then courteously desisted. Death can wait.
Powerless, with crude tears, we watched the cat
Totter and reassert itself again and again
Its life the fuel for its will to live
Until the bones appeared, blood dried in veins,
The pelt was ragbag remnants, the eyes gone out
And the wind's task was easy and the cat fell.

# Sad Memories

They tell me I am beautiful: they praise my silken hair,
My little feet that silently slip on from stair to stair:
They praise my pretty trustful face and innocent grey eye;
Fond hands caress me oftentimes, yet would that I might die!

Why was I born to be abhorred of man and bird and beast?
The bullfinch marks me stealing by, and straight his song hath ceased;
The shrewmouse eyes me shudderingly, then flees; and, worse than that,
The housedog he flees after me – why was I born a cat?

Men prize the heartless hound who quits dry-eyed his native land;
Who wags a mercenary tail and licks a tyrant hand.
The leal true cat they prize not, that if e'er compelled to roam
Still flies, when let out of the bag, precipitately home.

They call me cruel. Do I know if mouse or song-bird feels?
I only know they make me light and salutary meals:
And if, as 'tis my nature to, ere I devour I tease 'em,
Why should a low-bred gardener's boy pursue me with a besom?

Should china fall or chandeliers, or anything but stocks –
Nay stocks, when they're in flowerpots – the cat expects hard knocks:
Should ever anything be missed – milk, coals, umbrellas, brandy –
The cat's pitched into with a boot or anything that's handy . . .

'I remember, I remember,' how one night I 'fleeted by,'
And gained the blessed tiles and gazed into the cold clear sky.
'I remember, I remember,' how my little lovers came;
And there, beneath the crescent moon, play'd many a little game.

They fought – by good St Catherine, 'twas a fearsome sight to see
The coal-black crest, the glowering orbs, of one gigantic He.
Like bow by some tall bowman bent at Hastings or Poictiers,
His huge back curved, till none observed a vestige of his ears:

He stood, an ebon crescent, flouting that ivory moon;
Then raised the pibroch of his race, the Song without a Tune;
Gleam'd his white teeth, his mammoth tail waved darkly to and fro,
As with one complex yell he burst, all claws, upon the foe.

66

It thrills me now, that final miaow – that weird unearthly din:
Lone maidens heard it far away, and leapt out of their skin.
A potboy from his den o'erhead peep'd with a scared wan face;
Then sent a random brickbat down, which knocked me into space.

Nine days I fell, or thereabouts: and, had we not nine lives,
I wish I ne'er had seen again thy sausage-shop, St Ives!
Had I, as some cats have, nine tails, how gladly I would lick
The hand, and person generally, of him who heaved that brick!

For me they fill the milkbowl up, and cull the choice sardine;
But ah! I nevermore shall be the cat I once have been!
The memories of that fatal night they haunt me even now:
In dreams I see that rampant He, and tremble at that Miaow.

# The Auld Seceder Cat

There was a Presbyterian cat
Went forth to catch her prey;
She brought a mouse intill the house
Upon the Sabbath day.
The minister, offended
With such an act profane,
Laid down his book, the cat he took,
And bound her with a chain.

Thou vile malicious creature,
Thou murderer, said he,
Oh do you think to bring to Hell
My holy wife and me?
But be thou well assured
That blood for blood shall pay,
For taking of the mouse's life
Upon the Sabbath Day.

Then he took doun his Bible,
And fervently he prayed,
That the great sin the cat had done
Might not on him be laid.
Then forth to exe-cu-ti-on,
Poor Baudrons she was drawn,
And on a tree they hanged her hie,
And then they sang a psalm.

# The Death of a Cat

I

Since then, those months ago, these rooms miss something,
A link, a spark, and the street down there reproves
My negligence, particularly the gap
For the new block which, though the pile of timber
Is cleared on which he was laid to die, remains
A gap, a catch in the throat, a missing number.

You were away when I lost him, he had been absent
Six nights, two dead, which I had not learnt until
You returned and asked and found how he had come back
To a closed door having scoured the void of Athens
For who knows what and at length, more than unwell
Came back and less than himself, his life in tatters.

Since when I dislike that gap in the street and that obdurate
Dumb door of iron and glass and I resent
This bland blank room like a doctor's consulting room
With its too many exits, all of glass and frosted,
Through which he lurked and fizzed, a warm retort,
Found room for his bag of capers, his bubbling flasket.

For he was our puck, our miniature lar, he fluttered
Our dovecot of visiting cards, he flicked them askew,
The joker among them who made a full house. As you said,
He was a fine cat. Though how strange to have, as you said later,
Such a personal sense of loss. And looking aside
You said, but unconvincingly: What does it matter?

II

To begin with he was a beautiful object:
Blue crisp fur with a white collar,
Paws of white velvet, springs of steel,
A Pharaoh's profile, a Krishna's grace,
Tail like a questionmark at a masthead
And eyes dug out of a mine, not the dark
Clouded tarns of a dog's, but cat's eyes –
Light in a rock crystal, light distilled
Before his time and ours, before cats were tame.

To continue, he was alive and young,
A dancer, incurably male, a clown,
With his gags, his mudras, his entrechats,
His triple bends and his double takes,
Firm as a Rameses in African wonderstone,
Fluid as Krishna chasing the milkmaids,
Who hid under carpets and nibbled at olives,
Attacker of ankles, nonesuch of nonsense,
Indolent, impudent, cat catalytic.

To continue further: if not a person
More than a cipher, if not affectionate
More than indifferent, if not volitive
More than automaton, if not self-conscious
More than mere conscious, if not useful
More than a parasite, if allegorical
More than heraldic, if man-conditioned
More than a gadget, if perhaps a symbol
More than a symbol, if somewhat a proxy
More than a stand-in – was what he was!
A self-contained life, was what he must be
And is not now: more than an object.

And is not now. Spreadeagled on coverlets –
Those are the coverlets, bouncing on chairbacks –
These are the chairs, pirouetting and side-stepping,
Feinting and jabbing, breaking a picture-frame –
Here is the picture, tartar and sybarite,
One minute quicksilver, next minute butterballs,
Precise as a fencer, lax as an odalisque,
And in his eyes the light from the mines
One minute flickering, steady the next,
Lulled to a glow or blown to a blaze,
But always the light that was locked in the stone
Before his time and ours; at best semi-precious
All stones of that kind yet, if not precious,
Are more than stones, beautiful objects
But more than objects. While there is a light in them.

III

Canyons of angry sound, catastrophe, cataclysm,
Smells and sounds in cataracts, cat-Athens,
Not, not the Athens we know, each whisker buzzing
Like a whole Radar station, typhoons of grapeshot,
Crossfire from every roof of ultra-violet arrows
And in every gutter landmines, infra-red,
A massed barrage of too many things unknown
On too many too quick senses (cosseted senses
Of one as spoilt as Pangur Ban, Old Foss
Or My Cat Jeoffrey), all the drab and daily
Things to him deadly, all the blunt things sharp,
The paving-stones a sword dance. Chanting hawkers
Whose street cries consecrate their loaves and fishes
And huge black chessmen carved out of old priests
And steatopygous boys, they were all Gogs and Magogs
With seven-league battering boots and hair-on-ending voices
Through which he had to dodge. And all the wheels
Of all the jeeps, trucks, trams, motor-bicycles, buses, sports cars,
Caught in his brain and ravelled out his being
To one high horrible twang of breaking catgut,
A swastika of lightning. Such was Athens
To this one indoors cat, searching for what
He could not grasp through what he could not bear,
Dragged to and from by unseen breakers, broken
At last by something sudden: then dragged back
By his own obstinate instinct, a long dark thread
Like Ariadne's ball of wool in the labyrinth
Not now what he had played with as a kitten
But spun from his own catsoul, which he followed
Now that the minotaur of machines and men
Had gored him, followed it slowly, slowly, until
It snapped a few yards short of a closed door,
Of home, and he lay on his side like a fish on the pavement
While the ball of wool rolled back and down the hill,
His purpose gone, only his pain remaining
Which, even if purpose is too human a word,
Was not too human a pain for a dying cat.

Out of proportion? Why, almost certainly.
You and I, darling, knew no better
Than to feel worse for it. As one feels worse
When a tree is cut down, an ear-ring lost,
A week-end ended, a child at nurse
Weaned. Which are also out of proportion.

Sentimentality? Yes, it is possible;
You and I, darling, are not above knowing
The tears of the semi-, less precious things,
A pathetic fallacy perhaps, as the man
Who gave his marble victory wings
Was the dupe – who knows – of sentimentality.

Not really classic. The Greek Anthology
Laments its pets (like you and me, darling),
Even its grasshoppers; dead dogs bark
On the roads of Hades where poets hung
Their tiny lanterns to ease the dark.
Those poets were late though. Not really classical.

Yet more than an object? Why, most certainly.
You and I, darling, know that sonatas
Are more than sound and that green grass
Is more than grass or green, which is why
Each of our moments as they pass
Is of some moment; more than an object.

So this is an epitaph, not for calamitous
Loss but for loss; this was a person
In a small way who had touched our lives
With a whisk of delight, like a snatch of a tune
From which one whole day's mood derives.
For you and me, darling, this is an epitaph.

# Reprobates and Demons

Baudelaire tells us that cats take up *les nobles attitudes*. They rifle dustbins, too. The perfect example of the cat as sphinx-and-scapegrace is Mehitabel, the alley-cat who believes she is the reincarnation of Cleopatra. She is a lady, like Miss Ethel Merman's Edie (who had Class with a capital K) and she has as much personality as Sophie Tucker. This is a reprehensible lot, and one or two are plainly in league with fiends, especially in the frightening case of Edgar Allan Poe's Black Cat; although the narrator's autobiography does rouse the pro-fiend in one.

## An Alley Cat

Mangy and gaunt I walk the tiles tonight,
And mangy comes my lady to her tryst;
And nine lives back (nine hundred some have guessed)
With prouder mien we ramble, ranging light.
Sacred and sleek, on roofs of amethyst
And eaves of ivory we wandered while
A lotus-coloured moon swung up the Nile,
And Memphis slumbered in a silver mist.

O it was heaven just to sit and be
Antiphonal beneath some royal room
Until, for all our sacredness, we heard
Loud hieroglyphic curses flowing free,
And marked a sandal hurtling through the gloom
Hot from the hand of Rameses the Third.

# the song of mehitabel

this is the song of mehitabel
of mehitabel the alley cat
as i wrote you before boss
mehitabel is a believer
in the pythagorean
theory of the transmigration
of the souls and she claims
that formerly her spirit
was incarnated in the body
of cleopatra
that was a long time ago
and one must not be
surprised if mehitabel
has forgotten some of her
more regal manners

i have had my ups and downs
but wotthehell wotthehell
yesterday sceptres and crowns
fried oysters and velvet gowns
and today i herd with bums
but wotthehell wotthehell
i wake the world from sleep
as i caper and sing and leap
when i sing my wild free tune
wotthehell wotthehell
under the blear eyed moon
i am pelted with cast off shoon
but wotthehell wotthehell

do you think that i would change
my present freedom to range
for a castle or moated grange
wotthehell wotthehell
cage me and i d go frantic
my life is so romantic
capricious and corybantic
and i m toujours gai toujours gai

i know that i am bound
for a journey down the sound
in the midst of a refuse mound
but wotthehell wotthehell
oh i should worry and fret
death and i will coquette
there s a dance in the old dame yet
toujours gai toujours gai

i once was an innocent kit
wotthehell wotthehell
with a ribbon my neck to fit
and bells tied onto it
o wotthehell wotthehell
but a maltese cat came by
with a come hither look in his eye
and a song that soared to the sky
and wotthehell wotthehell
and i followed adown the street
the pad of his rhythmical feet
o permit me again to repeat
wotthehell wotthehell

my youth i shall never forget
but there s nothing i really regret
wotthehell wotthehell
there s a dance in the old dame yet
toujours gai toujours gai
the things that i had not ought to
i do because i ve gotto
wotthehell wotthehell
and i end with my favourite motto
toujours gai toujours gai

boss sometimes i think
that out friend mehitabel
is a trifle too gay

                    archy

# Cat!

Cat!
Scat!
Atter her, atter her,
Sleeky flatterer,
Spitfire chatterer,
Scatter her, scatter her
Off her mat!
*Wuff!*
*Wuff!*
Treat her rough!
Git her, git her,
Whiskery spitter!
Catch her, catch her,
Green-eyed scratcher!
Slathery
Slithery
Hisser,
Don't miss her!
Run till you're dithery,
Hithery
Thithery
*Pfitts! pfitts!*
How she spits!
Spitch! Spatch!
Can't she scratch!
Scritching the bark
Of the sycamore-tree,
She's reached her ark
And's hissing at me
*Pfitts! pfitts!*
*Wuff! wuff!*
Scat,
Cat!
That's
*That!*

# JOHN SKELTON

## A Curse on the Cat

Vengeance I ask and cry,
By way of exclamation
On all the whole nation
Of cats wild and tame;
God send them sorrow and shame!
That cat specially
That slew so cruelly
The little pretty sparrow
That I brought up at Carrow.
  O cat of churlish kind,
The fiend was in thy mind
When thou my bird untwind!
I would thou hadst been blind!
The leopards savage,
The lions in their rage,
Might catch thee in their paws,
And gnaw thee in their jaws!
The serpents of Libany
Might sting thee venomously!
The dragons with their tongues
Might poison thy liver and lungs!
The manticores of the mountains
Might feed them on thy brains!
  Melanchates, that hound
That plucked Actaeon to the ground,
Gave him his mortal wound,
Changed to a deer;
The story doth appear
Was changed to a hart:
So thou, foul cat that thou art,
The self same hound
Might thee confound,
That his own lord bote,
Might bite asunder thy throat!
Of Arcady the bears
Might pluck away thy ears!
The wild wolf Lycaon
Bite asunder thy back-bone!
Of Etna the burning hill,
That day and night burneth still,

Set thy tail in a blaze,
That all the world may gaze
And wonder upon thee,
From Ocean the great sea
Unto isles of Orkney,
From Tilbury ferry
To the plain of Salisbury!
So traitorously my bird to kill
That never owed thee evil will!

From *Lament for Philip Sparrow*

# The King o' the Cats

One winter's evening the sexton's wife was sitting by the fireside with her big black cat, Old Tom, on the other side, both half-asleep and waiting for the master to come home. They waited and they waited, but still he didn't come, till at last he came rushing in, calling out, 'Who's Tommy Tildrum?' in such a wild way that both his wife and his cat stared at him to know what was the matter.

'Why, what's the matter?' said his wife. 'And why do you want to know who Tommy Tildrum is?'

'Oh, I've had such an adventure. I was digging away at old Mr Fordyce's grave when I suppose I must have dropped asleep, and only woke up by hearing a cat's *Miaou.*'

'*Miaou!*' said Old Tom in answer.

'Yes, just like that! So I looked over the edge of the grave, and what do you think I saw?'

'Now, how can I tell?' said the sexton's wife.

'Why, nine black cats all like our friend Tom here, all with a white spot on their chestesses. And what do you think they were carrying? Why, a small coffin covered with a black velvet pall, and on the pall was a small coronet all of gold, and at every third step they took they cried altogether, *Miaou –*'

'*Miaou!*' said Old Tom again.

'Yes; just like that!' said the sexton. 'And as they came nearer and nearer to me I could see them more distinctly, because their eyes shone out with a sort of green light. Well, they all came towards me, eight of them carrying the coffin and the biggest cat of all walking in front for all the world like – But look at our Tom, how he's looking at me. You'd think he knew all I was saying.'

'Go on, go on,' said his wife; 'never mind Old Tom.'

'Well, as I was saying, they all came towards me slowly and solemnly, and at every third step crying altogether, *Miaou –*'

'*Miaou!*' said Old Tom again.

'Yes; just like that; till they came and stood right opposite Mr Fordyce's grave, where I was, when they all stood still and looked straight at me. I did feel queer, that I did! But look at Old Tom; he's looking at me just like they did.'

'Go on, go on,' said his wife; 'never mind Old Tom.'

'Where was I? Oh, they all stood still looking at me, when the one that wasn't carrying the coffin came forward and, staring straight at me, said to me – yes, I tell 'ee, *said* to me, – with a squeaky voice, "Tell Tom Tildrum that Tim Toldrum's dead," and that's why I asked you if you knew who

Tom Tildrum was, for how can I tell Tom Tildrum Tim Toldrum's dead if I don't know who Tom Tildrum is?'

'Look at Old Tom! Look at Old Tom!' screamed his wife.

And well he might look, for Tom was swelling, and Tom was staring, and at last Tom shrieked out, 'What – old Tim dead! Then I'm the King o' the Cats!' and rushed up the chimney and was never more seen.

From *A Dictionary of British Folk-Tales*

## The Tom-Cat

At midnight in the alley
   A Tom-cat comes to wail,
And he chants the hate of a million years
   As he swings his snaky tail.

Malevolent, bony, brindled,
   Tiger and devil and bard,
His eyes are coals from the middle of Hell
   And his heart is black and hard.

He twists and crouches and capers
   And bares his curved sharp claws,
And he sings to the stars of the jungle nights,
   Ere cities were, or laws.

Beast from a world primeval,
   He and his leaping clan,
When the blotched red moon leers over the roofs
   Give voice to their scorn of man.

He will lie on a rug tomorrow
   And lick his silky fur,
And veil the brute in his yellow eyes
   And play he's tame, and purr.

But at midnight in the alley
   He will crouch again and wail,
And beat the time for his demon's song
   With a swing of his demon's tail.

# To Mrs Reynolds's Cat

Cat! who hast past thy Grand Climacteric,
   How many mice and Rats hast in thy days
   Destroy'd? – how many titbits stolen? Gaze
With those bright languid segments green and prick
Those velvet ears – but pr'ythee do not stick
   Thy latent talons in me – and upraise
   Thy gentle mew – and tell me all thy phrase
Of Fish and Mice, and Rats and tender chick.
Nay look not down, nor lick thy dainty wrists –
   For all the wheezy Asthma, – and for all
Thy tail's tip is nipped off – and though the fuss
   Of many a Maid have given thee many a maul,
Still is that fur as soft as when the lists
   In youth thou enter'dst on glass-bottled wall.

## The Cat and the Lute

Are these the strings that poets say
Have cleared the air, and calmed the sea?
Charmed wolves, and from the mountain crests
Made forests dance with all their beasts?
Could these neglected shreds you see
Inspire a lute of ivory
And make it speak? Oh! think then what
Hath been committed by my cat,
Who, in the silence of this night
Hath gnawed these cords, and ruined them quite;
Leaving such remnants as may be
'Frets' – not for my lute, but me.

Puss, I will curse thee; mayest thou dwell
With some dry hermit in a cell
Where rat ne'er peeped, where mouse ne'er fed,
And flies go supperless to bed.
Or may'st thou tumble from some tower,
And fail to land upon all fours,
Taking a fall that may untie
Eight of nine lives, and let them fly.

What, was there ne'er a rat nor mouse,
Nor larder open? nought in the house
But harmless lute-strings could suffice
Thy paunch, and draw thy glaring eyes?

Know then, thou wretch, that every string
Is a cat-gut, which men do spin
Into a singing thread: think on that,
Thou cannibal, thou monstrous cat!

Thou seest, puss, what evil might betide thee:
But I forbear to hurt or chide thee:
For maybe puss was melancholy
And so to make her blithe and jolly
Finding these strings, she took a snatch
Of merry music: nay then, wretch,
Thus I revenge me, that as thou
Hast played on them, I've played on you.

# A Cat Exposes a Murderer

[*The narrator, his disposition worsened 'through the instrumentality of the Fiend Intemperance', kills his wife because she has stopped him killing his cat. He walls her body up in the cellar. The cat now disappears, and when the police search the house he feels quite safe. However . . .*]

'Gentlemen,' I said at last, as the party ascended the steps, 'I delight to have allayed your suspicions. I wish you all health and a little more courtesy. By the bye, gentlemen, this – this is a very well-constructed house,' (in the rabid desire to say something easily, I scarcely knew what I uttered at all), – 'I may say an *excellently* well-constructed house. These walls – are you going, gentlemen? – these walls are solidly put together'; and here, through the mere frenzy of bravado, I rapped heavily with a cane which I held in my hand, upon that very portion of the brickwork behind which stood the corpse of the wife of my bosom.

But may God shield me and deliver me from the fangs of the Arch-Fiend! No sooner had the reverberation of my blows sunk into silence, than I was answered by a voice from within the tomb! – by a cry, at first muffled, and broken, like the sobbing of a child, and then quickly swelling into one long, loud and continuous scream, utterly anomalous and in-human – a howl – a wailing shriek, half of horror and half of triumph, such as might have arisen only out of hell, conjointly from the throats of the damned in their agony and of the demons that exult in the damnation.

Of my own thought it is folly to speak. Swooning, I staggered to the opposite wall. For one instant the party on the stairs remained motionless, through extremity of terror and awe. In the next a dozen stout arms were toiling at the wall. It fell bodily. The corpse, already greatly decayed and clotted with gore, stood erect before the eyes of the spectators. Upon its head, with red extended mouth and solitary eye of fire, sat the hideous beast whose craft had seduced me into murder, and whose informing voice had consigned me to the hangman. I had walled the monster up within the tomb.

From *The Black Cat*

# Monsieur Pussy-Cat, Blackmailer

*C'est un grand Monsieur* Pussy-Cat
Who lives on the mat
*Devant un feu énorme*
And that is why he is so fat,
*En effet il sait quelque chose*
*Et fait chanter son hôte,*
*Raison de plus pourquoi*
He has such a glossy coat.
*Ah ha, Monsieur* Pussy-Cat,
*Si grand et si gras,*
Take care you don't *pousser trop*
The one who gives you such *jolis plats.*

# A Cat's Conscience

A Dog will often steal a bone,
But conscience lets him not alone,
And by his tail his guilt is known.

But cats consider theft a game,
And, howsoever you may blame,
Refuse the slightest sign of shame.

When food mysteriously goes,
The chances are that Pussy knows
More than she leads you to suppose.

And hence there is no need for you,
If Puss declines a meal or two,
To feel her pulse and make ado.

## I. A. KRYLOV

# The Cat and the Cook

A cook, a literate man,
left his cookhouse
for the tavern. (He was a religious man,
and on that day he was leading a memorial wake for his grandfather),
and at home, to guard edibles from mice,
he left a cat.
But what, on his return, does he see? On the floor
the remains of the pie; and Basil Cat in the corner,
curled up behind the vinegar-barrel,
growling and purring, is busy with a chicken.
'Oh, you glutton, oh, villain –'
– now the cook scolds Basil –
'aren't you ashamed of yourself, like a human being?'
(Meanwhile Basil just keeps taking the chicken apart)
'What! You've been an honest cat up till now;
– people used to point to you as an example of a gentleman –
– and now you . . . Alas! what shame.
Now all my neighbours will say:
"Basil the cat is a rogue! Basil the cat is a thief!
That Basil shouldn't be let into the cookhouse
or even into the yard,
like a hungry wolf to the cattle food
he's corruption, he's the plague, he's a pestilence in these places!"'
(Meanwhile Basil listens, and eats.)
Here my orator, having let his flow of words have its will,
could not fit a suitable end to his moralising speech.
But what of it? While he chanted it,
Basil the cat ate up the whole roast.
And I would tell another cook
to carve on the wall
that he shouldn't waste speeches
when he should be using force.

*Translated from the Russian by Paul Snowden*

## That Cat

The cat that comes to my window-sill
When the moon looks cold and the night is still –
He comes in a frenzied state alone
With a tail that stands like a pine-tree cone,
And says 'I have finished my evening lark,
And I think I can hear a hound dog bark.
My whiskers are froze 'nd stuck to my chin.
I do wish you'd git up and let me in.'
    That cat gits in.

But if in the solitude of the night
He doesn't appear to be feeling right,
And rises and stretches and seeks the floor,
And some remote corner he would explore,
And doesn't feel satisfied just because
There's no good spot for to sharpen his claws,
And Meows and canters uneasy about
Beyond the least shadow of any doubt
    That cat gits out.

# From Sophisti-Cats

Don't never cross a road what a black cat
cross't aint nothing but sorrow, 't aint
nothing but loss.
Brindle cat, spotted cat, dem's all right;
Safety in a yaller cat, blessin' in a white;
But de black cat ructious, wid a bristle in his tail,
He fotchin' for de Debble, and he better not fail.
De black cat travel wid his belly in de dus';
He gwine whar he gwine, and he gwine kase he mus'.
Black cat, black cat – when he cross yo track,
No matter whar yo gwine,
To a dippin' or a dyin',
No matter whar yo hurryin'
To a marryin' or a buryin' –
    You better turn back!

# Mystics

Ineffable, effable,
Effanineffable
Deep and inscrutable
Singular . . .

says T. S. Eliot (see 'The Naming of Cats' in the next
section) and it is agreed by the writers in this section, a
galaxy of genius, that the cat is a mystery, and an agent
of the occult. There is a fine line between these Mystics
and the Demons of the last section – Ruth Pitter's
*Quorum Porum* are as sinister as Macbeth's witches – the
distinction is that this section dwells on their state and
not on their deeds. Some might question the presence of
the Cheshire Cat, that dispassionate logician, in this
company; but as he can disappear and leave his grin behind,
he is plainly a highly advanced Yogi and a true mystic.

## Les Chats

Les amoureux fervents et les savants austères
Aiment également, dans leur mûre saison,
Les chats puissants et doux, orgueil de la maison,
Qui comme eux sont frileux et comme eux sédentaires.

Amis de la science et de la volupté,
Ils cherchent le silence et l'horreur des ténèbres;
L'Erèbe les eût pris pour ses coursiers funèbres,
S'ils pouvaient au servage incliner leur fierté.

Ils prennent en songeant les nobles attitudes
Des grands sphinx allongés au fond des solitudes,
Qui semblent s'endormir dans un rêve sans fin;

Leurs reins féconds sont pleins d'étincelles magiques,
Et des parcelles d'or, ainsi qu'un sable fin,  ·
Etoilent vaguement leurs prunelles mystiques.

# Cats

Passionate lovers and ascetic old
philosophers, – these two appreciate best
the charm of cats, sedate and self-possessed,
like both these sedentary and hating cold.

The learned and the sensual they befriend,
loving quiet and darkness where temptation breeds;
Erebus would make them his funeral steeds
if to subjection they would condescend.

Like age-old sphinxes crouched upon the sand,
they strike majestic attitudes to dream
and gaze at nothingness, detached and wise:

with volted sparks their fruitful loins expand,
and golden particles of star-dust stream
like endless comets from their secret eyes.

*Translation by Wrenne Jarman*

# Cat

Dear creature by the fire a-purr,
   Strange idol, eminently bland,
Miraculous puss! As o'er your fur
   I trail a negligible hand,

And gaze into your gazing eyes,
   And wonder in a demi-dream
What mystery it is that lies
   Behind those slits that glare and gleam,

An exquisite enchantment falls
   About the portals of my sense;
Meandering through enormous halls
   I breathe luxurious frankincense,

An ampler air, a warmer June
   Enfold me, and my wondering eye
Salutes a more imperial moon
   Throned in a more resplendent sky

Than ever knew this northern shore.
   Oh, strange! For you are with me too,
And I who am a cat once more
   Follow the woman that was you

With tail erect and pompous march,
   The proudest puss that ever trod,
Through many a grove, 'neath many an arch,
   Impenetrable as a god,

Down many an alabaster flight
   Of broad and cedar-shaded stairs,
While over us the elaborate night
   Mysteriously gleams and glares!

# Alice Talks to the Cheshire Cat

The cat only grinned when it saw Alice. It looked good-natured, she thought: still it had *very* long claws and a great many teeth, so she felt that it ought to be treated with respect.

'Cheshire puss,' she began, rather timidly, as she did not at all know whether it would like the name: however, it only grinned a little wider. 'Come, it's pleased so far,' thought Alice, and she went on. 'Would you tell me, please, which way I ought to go from here?'

'That depends a good deal on where you want to get to,' said the Cat.

'I don't much care where –' said Alice.

'Then it doesn't matter which way you go,' said the Cat.

'– so long as I get *somewhere*,' Alice added as an explanation.

'Oh, you're sure to do that,' said the Cat, 'if you walk long enough.'

Alice felt that this could not be denied, so she tried another question. 'What sort of people live about here?'

'In *that* direction,' said the Cat, waving its right paw round, 'lives a Hatter: and in *that* direction,' waving the other paw, 'lives a March Hare. Visit either you like: they're both mad.'

'But I don't want to go among mad people,' Alice remarked.

'Oh, you can't help that,' said the Cat: 'we're all mad here. I'm mad. You're mad.'

'How do you know I'm mad?' said Alice.

'You must be,' said the Cat, 'or you wouldn't have come here.'

Alice didn't think that proved it at all: however she went on: 'And how do you know that you're mad?'

'To begin with,' said the Cat, 'a dog's not mad. You grant that?'

'I suppose so,' said Alice.

'Well, then,' the Cat went on, 'you see a dog growls when it's angry, and wags its tail when it's pleased. Now *I* growl when I'm pleased, and wag my tail when I'm angry. Therefore I'm mad.'

'*I* call it purring, not growling,' said Alice.

'Call it what you like,' said the Cat. 'Do you play croquet with the Queen today?'

'I should like it very much,' said Alice, 'but I haven't been invited yet.'

'You'll see me there,' said the Cat, and vanished.

Alice was not much surprised at this, she was getting so used to queer things happening. While she was still looking at the place where it had been, it suddenly appeared again.

'By-the-bye, what became of the baby?' said the Cat. 'I'd nearly forgotten to ask.'

'It turned into a pig,' Alice answered very quietly, just as if the Cat had come back in a natural way.

'I thought it would,' said the Cat, and vanished again.

Alice waited a little, half expecting to see it again, but it did not appear, and after a minute or two she walked on in the direction in which the March Hare was said to live. 'I've seen hatters before,' she said to herself: 'the March Hare will be much the more interesting, and perhaps, as this is May, it won't be raving mad – at least not so mad as it was in March.' As she said this, she looked up, and there was the Cat again, sitting on the branch of a tree.

'Did you say "pig", or "fig"?' said the Cat.

'I said "pig",' replied Alice, 'and I wish you wouldn't keep appearing and vanishing so suddenly: you make one quite giddy!'

'All right,' said the Cat; and this time it vanished quite slowly, beginning with the end of the tail, and ending with the grin, which remained some time after the rest of it had gone.

'Well! I've often seen a cat without a grin,' thought Alice; 'but a grin without a cat! It's the most curious thing I ever saw in all my life!'

From *Alice in Wonderland*

# Of Cats

A heart constituted wholly of cats
(Even as the family nose derives)
From father and mother a child inherits,
And every cat gets fully nine lives.

Wildest cats, with scruff cats, queenly cats
(Crowned), they jig to violins; they go stately
Where a torched pageantry celebrates
A burial, or crowning (of a cat); or sing sweetly.

At your ears and in harmony left with right
Till the moon bemoods: to the new, to the full,
Only look up: possessing night –
Cattic Bacchanal! A world of wild lamps and wauling,

A world gone to the cats, every cat of the heart out,
And darkness and light a cat upon a cat – .
They have outwitted our nimblest wits.
One who, one night, sank a cat in a sack

With a stone to the canal-bottom
(Under the bridge, in the very belly of the black)
And hurried a mile home
Found that cat on the doorstep waiting for him.

So are we all held in utter mock by the cats.

# Femme et Chatte

They were at play, she and her cat,
And it was marvellous to mark
The white paws and the white hand pat
Each other in the deepening dark.

The stealthy little lady hid
Under her mittens' silken sheath
Her deadly agate nails that thrid
The silk-like dagger-points of death.

The cat purred primly and drew in
Her claws that were of steel filed thin:
The devil was in it all the same.

And in the boudoir, while a shout
Of laughter in the air rang out,
Four sparks of phosphor shone like flame.

*From the French of Paul Verlaine*

# The Mysterious Cat

I saw a proud, mysterious cat,
I saw a proud, mysterious cat,
Too proud to catch a mouse or a rat –
Mew, mew, mew.

But catnip she would eat, and purr,
But catnip she would eat, and purr.
And goldfish she did much prefer –
Mew, mew, mew.

I saw a cat – 'twas but a dream,
I saw a cat – 'twas but a dream,
Who scorned the slave who brought her cream –
Mew, mew, mew.

Unless the slave were dressed in style,
Unless the slave were dressed in style,
And knelt before her all the while –
Mew, mew, mew.

Did you ever hear of a thing like that?
Did you ever hear of a thing like that?
Did you ever hear of a thing like that?
Oh, what a proud mysterious cat.
Oh, what a proud mysterious cat.
Oh, what a proud mysterious cat.
Mew, mew, mew.

# The Cat-Headed Goddess of the Moon

As the cat sees in darkness, so the sun, which journeyed into the under-world at night, saw through its gloom. Bast was the representative of the moon, because that planet was considered as the sun god's eye during the hours of darkness. For as the sun reflects the light of the solar system, so the cat's phosphorescent eyes were held to mirror the sun's rays when it was otherwise invisible to man. Bast, as the cat-moon, held the sun in her eyes during the night, keeping watch with the light he bestowed upon her, whilst her paws gripped and bruised and pierced the head of his deadly enemy, the serpent of darkness. Thus she justified her title of tearer and render and proved it was not incompatible with love.

From *The Cat in the Mysteries of Religion and Magic*

# The Cat and the Moon

The cat went here and there
And the moon spun round like a top,
And the nearest kin of the moon,
The creeping cat, looked up.
Black Minnaloushe stared at the moon,
For, wander and wail as he would,
The pure cold light in the sky
Troubled his animal blood.
Minnaloushe runs in the grass
Lifting his delicate feet.
Do you dance, Minnaloushe, do you dance?
When two close kindred meet,
What better than call a dance?
Maybe the moon may learn,
Tired of that courtly fashion,
A new dance turn.
Minnaloushe creeps through the grass
From moonlit place to place,
The sacred moon over head
Has taken a new phase.
Does Minnaloushe know that his pupils
Will pass from change to change,
And that from round to crescent,
From crescent to round they range?
Minnaloushe creeps through the grass
Alone, important and wise,
And lifts to the changing moon
His changing eyes.

# The Cat

Within that porch, across the way,
I see two naked eyes this night;
Two eyes that neither shut nor blink,
Searching my face with a green light.

But cats to me are strange, so strange –
I cannot sleep if one is near;
And though I'm sure I see those eyes,
I'm not so sure a body's there!

## *From* A Conversation with a Cat

[*The author has sat down in the bar of a railway station 'to meditate upon the necessary but tragic isolation of the human soul', when a beautiful, tawny cat jumps on his lap. He calls her Amathea.*]

'I am more than flattered, Amathea,' said I, . . . 'I am consoled. I did not know that there was in the world anything breathing and moving, let alone one so tawny-perfect, who would give companionship for its own sake and seek out, through deep feeling, some one companion out of all living kind. If you do not address me in words I know the reason and commend it; for in words lie the deeds of all dissension, and love at its most profound is silent. At least, I read that in a book, Amathea; yes, only the other day. But I confess that the book told me nothing of those gestures which are better than words, or of that caress which I continue to bestow upon you with all the gratitude of my poor heart.'

. . . Amathea slowly raised herself upon her four feet, arched her back, yawned, looked up at me with a smile sweeter than ever and then went round and round, preparing for herself a new couch upon my coat, whereon she settled and began once more to purr in settled ecstasy.

Already had I made sure that a rooted and anchored affection had come to me from out the emptiness and nothingness of the world and was to feed my soul henceforth; already had I changed the mood of long years and felt a conversion towards the life of things, an appreciation, a cousinship with the created light – and all that through one new link of loving kindness – when whatever it is that dashes the cup of bliss from the lips of mortal man (Tupper) up and dashed it good and hard. It was the Ancient Enemy who put the fatal sentence into my heart, for we are the playthings of the greater powers, and surely some of them are evil.

'You will never leave me, Amathea,' I said; 'I will respect your sleep and we will sit here together through all uncounted time, I holding you in my arms and you dreaming of the fields of Paradise. Nor shall anything part us, Amathea; you are my cat and I am your human. Now and onwards into the fullness of peace.'

Then it was that Amathea lifted herself once more, and with delicate, discreet, unweighted movement of perfect limbs leapt lightly to the floor as lovely as a wave. She walked slowly away from me without so much as looking back over her shoulder; she had another purpose in her mind; and as she so gracefully and so majestically neared the door which she was seeking, a short, unpleasant man standing at the bar said, 'Puss, Puss, Puss!' and stooped to scratch her gently behind the ear. With what a wealth of singular affection, pure and profound, did she not gaze up at him, and then rub herself against his leg in token and external expression of a sacramental friendship that should never die.

## London Tom-Cat

Look at the gentle savage, monstrous gentleman
With jungles in his heart, yet metropolitan
As we shall never be; who – while his human hosts,
Afraid of their own past and its primaeval ghosts,
Pile up great walls for comfort – walks coquettishly
Through their elaborate cares, sure of himself and free
To be like them, domesticated, or aloof!
A dandy in the room, a demon on the roof,
He's delicately tough, endearingly reserved,
Adaptable, fastidious, rope-and-fibre nerved.
Now an accomplished Yogi good at sitting still
He ponders ancient mysteries on the window-sill,
Now stretches, bares his claws and saunters off to find
The thrills of love and hunting, cunningly combined.
Acrobat, diplomat, and simple tabby-cat,
He conjures tangled forests in a furnished flat.

# On a Night of Snow

Cat, if you go outdoors you must walk in the snow,
You will come back with little white shoes on your feet,
Little white slippers of snow that have heels of sleet.
Stay by the fire, my Cat. Lie still, do not go.
See how the flames are leaping and hissing low,
I will bring you a saucer of milk like a marguerite,
So white and so smooth, so spherical and so sweet –
Stay with me, Cat. Out-doors the wild winds blow.

Out-doors the wild winds blow, Mistress, and dark is the night.
Strange voices cry in the trees, intoning strange lore,
And more than cats move, lit by our eyes' green light,
On silent feet where the meadow grasses hang hoar –
Mistress, there are portents abroad of magic and might,
And things that are yet to be done. Open the door!

# Effect of the Cat Webster on Lancelot Mulliner

[*Lancelot Mulliner, a Bohemian artist, is engaged to marry another Bohemian artist. But the cat Webster, whom he is minding for his uncle, a Dean, is exerting a sinister influence on him.*]

'Come, old man,' said Scollop, laying a gentle hand on Lancelot's bowed shoulder. 'We are your friends. Confide in us.'

'Tell us all,' said Worple. 'What's the matter?"

Lancelot uttered a bitter, mirthless laugh.

'You want to know what's the matter? Listen, then. I'm cat-pecked!'

'Cat-pecked?'

'You've heard of men being hen-pecked, haven't you?' said Lancelot with a touch of irritation. 'Well, I'm cat-pecked.'

And in broken accents he told his story. He sketched the history of his association with Webster from the latter's first entry into the studio. Confident now that the animal was not within earshot, he unbosomed himself without reserve.

'It's something in the beast's eye,' he said in a shaking voice. 'Something hypnotic. He casts a spell upon me. He gazes at me and disapproves. Little by little, bit by bit, I am degenerating under his influence from a wholesome, self-respecting artist into . . . well, I don't know what you call it. Suffice it to say that I have given up smoking, that I have ceased to wear carpet slippers and go about without a collar, that I never dream of sitting down to my frugal evening meal without dressing, and' – he choked – 'I have sold my ukulele.'

'Not that!' said Worple, paling.

'Yes,' said Lancelot. 'I felt he considered it frivolous.'

There was a long silence.

'Mulliner,' said Scollop, 'this is more serious than I had supposed. We must brood upon your case.'

'It may be possible,' said Worple, 'to find a way out.'

Lancelot shook his head hopelessly.

'There is no way out. I have explored every avenue. The only thing that could possibly free me from this intolerable bondage would be if once – just once – I could catch that cat unbending. If once – merely once – it would lapse in my presence from its austere dignity for but a single instant, I feel that the spell would be broken. But what hope is there of that?' cried Lancelot passionately. 'You were pointing just now to that alley cat in the yard. There stands one who has strained every nerve and spared no effort to break down Webster's inhuman self-control. I have heard that animal say things to him which you would think no cat with red blood in its veins would suffer for an instant. And Webster merely looks at him like a Suffragan Bishop eyeing an erring choir-boy and turns his head and falls into a refreshing sleep.'

He broke off with a dry sob. Worple, always an optimist, attempted in his kindly way to minimize the tragedy.

'Ah, well,' he said. 'It's bad, of course, but still, I suppose there is no actual harm in shaving and dressing for dinner and so on. Many great artists . . . Whistler, for example—'

'Wait!' cried Lancelot. 'You have not heard the worst.'

He rose feverishly, and, going to the easel, disclosed the portrait of Brenda Carberry-Pirbright.

'Take a look ar her,' he said, 'and tell me what you think of her.'

His two friends surveyed the face before them in silence. Miss Carberry-Pirbright was a young woman of prim and glacial aspect. One sought in vain for her reasons for wanting to have her portrait painted. It would be a most unpleasant thing to have about any house.

Scollop broke the silence.

'Friend of yours?'

'I can't stand the sight of her,' said Lancelot vehemently.

'Then,' said Scollop, 'I may speak frankly. I think she's a pill.'

'A blister,' said Worple.

'A boil and a disease', said Scollop, summing up.

Lancelot laughed hackingly.

'You have described her to a nicety. She stands for everything most alien to my artist soul. She gives me a pain in the neck. I'm going to marry her.'

'What!' cried Scollop.

'But you're going to marry Gladys Bingley,' said Worple.

'Webster thinks not,' said Lancelot bitterly.

From *The Story of Webster*

# Why He Stroked the Cats

He stroked the cats on account of a specific cause,
Namely, when he entered the house he felt
That the floor might split and the four walls suddenly melt
In strict accord with certain magic laws
That, it seemed, the carving over the front door meant,
Laws violated when men like himself stepped in,

But he had nothing to lose and nothing to win,
So in he always stepped. Before him went
Always his shadow. The sun was at his back.

The ceilings were high and the passageway was so black
That he welcomed the great cats who advanced to meet him,
The two of them arching their soft high backs to greet him;

He would kneel and stroke them gently under their jaws,
All that is mentioned above being the cause.

# Quorum Porum*

In a dark garden, by a dreadful tree,
The Druid Toms were met. They numbered three,
Tab Tiger, Demon Black, and Ginger Hate.
Their forms were tense, their eyes were full of fate;
Save the involuntary caudal thrill,
The horror was that they should sit so still.
An hour of ritual silence passed: then low
And marrow-freezing, Ginger moaned 'OROW',
Two horrid syllables of hellish lore,
Followed by deeper silence than before.
Another hour, the tabby's turn is come;
Rigid, he rapidly howls 'MUM MUM MUM';
Then reassumes his silence like a pall,
Clothed in negation, a dumb oracle.
At the third hour, the black gasps out 'AH BLURK!'
Like a lost soul that flounders in the murk;
And the grim, ghastly, damned and direful crew
Resumes its voiceless vigilance anew.
The fourth hour passes. Suddenly all three
Chant 'WEGGY WEGGY WEGGY' mournfully,
Then stiffly rise, and melt into the shade,
Their Sabbath over, and their demons laid.

*Porum – Genitive plural of 'Puss'.

# The Nature of the Creature

Cats do not intend to be understood, and so these pieces study them not as a whole but from various angles, as the blind men did the elephant. But perverse, evasive, atavistic, his mind on the moon (or the thought, the thought, the thought of his name), resounding, when happy, 'with an enclosed and private sound', the cat is for certain a wonderful stimulus to his literary admirers.

# The Nature of the Creature

Lat take a cat, and fostre him well with milk,
And tendre flesh, and make his couch of silk,
And lat him see a mous go by the wall;
Anon he weyveth milk, and flesh, and al
And every deyntee that is in that hous,
Swich appetyt hath he to ete a mous . . .

From *The Canterbury Tales*

# Cats

Cats no less liquid than their shadows
Offer no angles to the wind.
They slip, diminished, neat, through loopholes
Less than themselves; will not be pinned

To rules or routes for journeys; counter
Attack with non-resistance; twist
Enticing through the curving fingers
And leave an angered, empty fist.

They wait obsequious as darkness
Quick to retire, quick to return;
Admit no aim or ethics; flatter
With reservations; will not learn

To answer to their names; are seldom
Truly owned till shot or skinned
Cats, no less liquid than their shadows
Offer no angles to the wind.

# Cat-Goddesses

A perverse habit of cat-goddesses –
Even the best of them, black as coals
Save for a new moon blazing on each breast,
With coral tongues and beryl eyes like lamps,
Long-legged, pacing three by three in nines –
This obstinate habit is to yield themselves,
In verisimilar love-ecstasies,
To tatter-eared and slinking alley-toms,
No less below the common run of cats
Than they above it; which they do for spite,
To provoke jealousy – not the least abashed
By such gross-headed, rabbit-coloured litters
As soon they shall be happy to desert.

## Esther's Tomcat

Daylong this tomcat lies stretched flat
As an old rough mat, no mouth and no eyes.
Continual wars and wives are what
Have tattered his ears and battered his head.

Like a bundle of old rope and iron
Sleeps till blue dusk. Then reappear
His eyes, green as ringstones; he yawns wide red,
Fangs fine as a lady's needle and bright.

A tomcat sprang at a mounted knight,
Locked round his neck like a trap of hooks
While the knight rode fighting its clawing and bite.
After hundreds of years the stain's there

On the stone where he fell, dead of the tom:
That was at Barnborough. The tomcat still
Grallochs odd dogs on the quiet,
Will take the head clean off your simple pullet,

Is unkillable. From the dog's fury,
From gunshot fired point-blank he brings
His skin whole, and whole
From owlish moons and bekittenings

Among ashcans. He leaps and lightly
Walks upon sleep, his mind on the moon.
Nightly over the round world of men
Over the roofs go his eyes and outcry.

# The Prize Cat

Pure blooded domestic, guaranteed,
Soft-mannered, musical in purr,
The ribbon had declared the breed,
Gentility was in the fur.

Such feline culture in the gads,
No anger ever arched her back –
What distance since those velvet pads
Departed from the leopard's track!

And when I mused how Time had thinned
The jungle strains within the cells,
How human hands had disciplined
Those prowling optic parallels;

I saw the generations pass
Along the reflex of a spring,
A bird had rustled in the grass,
The tab had caught it on the wing:

Behind the leap so furtive-wild
Was such ignition in the gleam,
I thought an Abyssinian child
Had cried out in the whitethroat's scream.

# Ailurophobe and Ailurophile

A person who actually does not like cats is called an ailurophobe, and will quite likely go to his tomb without ever knowing that Turkish cats like swimming, that blue-eyed whites are usually deaf, that when the Earl of Southampton was imprisoned in the Tower his cat came down the chimney to him, that a cat called 'Pussycat' fell 120 feet from a block of flats in Maida Vale on March 7th 1965 and landed unhurt, that 100,000 cats are employed by the British Civil Service, that 'tabby' was the name for a striped silk made in *Attabiy*, a quarter of Baghdad named after Attab, son of Omeyya, and that is why striped cats are called tabbies.

A cat-lover, or ailurophile, would of course prefer to think that the striped silk was named after the cat, and that Tibshelf, a village in Derbyshire, is a natural rock shelf lined with huge cats like those still seen on the window-sills of St Ives, in the houses which have window-sills large enough. This is unfortunately not true. However, it is a simple matter to call the shelf on which your cats like to sleep, high up out of the reach of people, when it is too wet to scrabble up 60-foot trees, the tibshelf.

Even in households where an ailurophobe is married to an ailurophile it is fairly likely that there will be more than one cat. It is very hard to have just one cat. This is not only because it is perfectly possible for you to have a kitten who starts peering in all your cupboards after you have had her for ten days, looking for places to have the kittens that she is already carrying, and will shortly have with the utmost nonchalance, leaving absolutely no mess, just these three slightly smaller kittens, before you have even begun to think about 'taking her to the vet', as ailurophobes put it. You may, for instance, have a tom who was taken to the vet years ago, and now looks like Osmin, the enormous guardian of the harem in Mozart's opera *Il Seraglio*. 'He is getting old,' you will find yourself saying (even if you are the ailurophobe), 'it will be awful when he dies, let's get another one and sort of play it in.'

# Catalogue

Cats sleep fat and walk thin.
Cats, when they sleep, slump;
When they wake, pull in –
And where the plump's been
There's skin.
Cats walk thin.

Cats wait in a jump,
Jump in a streak.
Cats, when they jump, are sleek
As a grape slipping its skin –
They have technique.
Oh, cats don't creak.
They sneak.

Cats sleep fat.
They spread comfort beneath them
Like a good mat,
As if they picked the place
And then sat.
You walk around one
As if he were the City Hall
After that.

If male,
A cat is apt to sing upon a major scale:
This concert is for everybody, this
Is wholesale.
For a baton, he wields a tail.

(He is also found,
When happy, to resound
With an enclosed and private sound.)

A cat condenses.
He pulls in his tail to go under bridges,
And himself to go under fences.
Cats fit
In any size box or kit;
And if a large pumpkin grew under one,
He could arch over it.

When everyone else is just ready to go out,
The cat is just ready to come in.
He's not where he's been.
Cats sleep fat and walk thin.

# Peter

Strong and slippery, built for the midnight grass-party confronted by
                                                    four cats,
    he sleeps his time away – the detached first claw on the foreleg, which
                                                    corresponds
        to the thumb, retracted to its tip; the small tuft of fronds
        or katydid-legs above each eye, still numbering the unit in each
                                                    group;
            the shadbones regularly set about the mouth, to droop or rise

in unison like the porcupine's quills – motionless. He lets himself be flat-
    tened out by gravity, as it were a piece of seaweed tamed and
                                                    weakened by
        exposure to the sun; compelled when extended, to lie
        stationary. Sleep is the result of his delusion that one must do as
            well as one can for oneself; sleep – epitome of what is to

him as to the average person, the end of life. Demonstrate on him how
    the lady caught the dangerous southern snake, placing a forked stick
                                                    on either
        side of its innocuous neck; one need not try to stir
        him up; his prune-shaped head and alligator eyes are not a party to
                                                    the
            joke. Lifted and handled, he may be dangled like an eel or set

up on the forearm like a mouse; his eyes bisected by pupils of a pin's
    width, are flickeringly exhibited, then covered up. May be? I should
                                                    say
        might have been; when he has been got the better of in a
        dream– as in a fight with nature or with cats – we all know it.
                                    Profound sleep is
            not with him a fixed illusion. Springing about with frog-like ac-

curacy, emitting jerky cries when taken in the hand, he is himself
    again; to sit caged by the rungs of a domestic chair would be unprofit-
    able – human. What is the good of hypocrisy? It
        is permissible to choose one's employment, to abandon the wire
                                                    nail, the
            roly-poly, when it shows signs of being no longer a pleas-

ure, to score the adjacent machine with a double line of strokes. He can
talk, but insolently says nothing. What of it? When one is frank, one's
                                                              very
presence is a compliment. It is clear that he can see
        the virtue of naturalness, that he is one of those who do not regard
        the published fact as a surrender. As for the disposition

invariably to affront, an animal with claws wants to have to use
        them; that eel-like extension of trunk into tail is not an accident. To
leap, to lengthen out, divide the air – to purloin, to pursue.
        To tell the hen: fly over the fence, go in the wrong way in your
                                                              perturba-
        tion – this is life; to do less would be nothing but dishonesty.

# White Cats

*(To Albert Dugrip)*

In the clear gold of sunlight, stretching their backs,
– White as snow – see the voluptuous cats,
Closing eyes jealous of their inner glooms,
Slumbering in the tepid warmth of their illumined fur.

Their coats have the dazzle of dawn-bathed glaciers.
Inside them, their bodies, frail, sinewy, and slender,
Feel the shiverings of a girl inside her dress,
And their beauty refines itself in endless languors.

No question but their Soul of old has animated
The flesh of a philosopher, or a woman's body,
For since then their dazzling and inestimable whiteness

Holding the mingled splendour of a grand premiere,
Ennobles them to a rank of calm contempt,
Indifferent to everything but *Light* itself!

*From the French of Paul Valery*

## Cat Into Lady

A man possessed a Cat on which he doted.
So fine she was, so soft, so silky-coated –
Her very mew had quality!
He was as mad as mad could be.
　So one fine day, by dint of supplications,
And tears, and charms, and conjurations,
He worked upon the Powers above
To turn her woman; and the loon
Took her to wife that very afternoon.
Before, 'twas findness crazed him: now 'twas love!
Never did peerless beauty fire
Her suitor with more wild desire
Than this unprecedented spouse
Th'eccentric partner of her vows.
They spend their hours in mutual coaxing,
He sees each day less trace of cat,
And lastly, hoaxed beyond all hoaxing,
Deems her sheer woman, through and through;
Till certain mice, who came to gnaw the mat,
Disturbed the couple at their bill-and-coo.
The wife leapt up – but missed her chance;
And soon, their fears allayed by her new guise,
The mice crept back: this time she was in stance,
And took 'em by surprise.
Thenceforth all means were unavailing
T'eradicate her little failing.

The bent we are born with rules us till we die.
It laughs at schooling: by a certain age
The vessel smacks, the stuff has ta'en its ply.
Man strives in vain to disengage
His will from this necessity.
Our nature, so confirmed by use,
Binds us in chains that none may loose:
Whips and scorpions, brands and burns,
Leave it as it was before:
If you drive it through the door
By the window it returns.

*Translated from the French by Sir Edward Marsh*

## The Cat

Hark! She is calling to her cat.
She is down the misty garden in a tatter-brim straw hat,
And broken slippers grass-wet, treading fearful daisies.
But he does not heed her. He sits still – and gazes.

Where the laden gooseberry leans over to the rose,
He sits thorn-protected, gazing down his nose.
Coffee-coloured skies above him press upon the sun;
Bats about his mistress flitter-flutter one by one;

Jessamines drop perfume; the nightingales begin;
Nightjars wind their humdrum notes; a crescent moon rides thin;
The daybird chorus dies away, the air shrinks chill and grey.
Her lonely voice still calls him – but her panther won't come in!

## Cat in the Long Grass

Seeing the size, the domed
depth of a cat's ear, the sensitive
membrane furred over
with fine curls,
I am surprised he walks
a true wild tiger
through the long grass
and its spears of seeds,
and how (wrong-toothed) he eats
the long grass, or chews
and merely plays with it,
startling a safe-seeming moth –
a grey charred paper
lifting from his fire.

## Man and Beast

Hugging the ground by the lilac tree,
With shadows in conspiracy,

The black cat from the house next door
Waits with death in each bared claw

For the tender unwary bird
That all the summer I have heard

In the orchard singing. I hate
The cat that is its savage fate,

And choose a stone with which to send
Slayer, not victim, to its end.

I look to where the black cat lies,
But drop my stone, seeing its eyes –

Who is it sins now, those eyes say,
You the hunter, or I the prey?

# Cat

The fat cat on the mat
　　may seem to dream
of nice mice that suffice
　　for him, or cream;
but he free, maybe,
　　walks in thought
unbowed, proud, where loud
　　roared and fought
his kin, lean and slim,
　　or deep in den
in the East feasted on beasts
　　and tender men.

The giant lion with iron
　　claw in paw,
and huge ruthless tooth
　　in gory jaw;
the pard dark-starred,
　　fleet upon feet,
that oft soft from aloft
　　leaps on his meat
where woods loom in gloom –
　　far now they be,
　　fierce and free,
　　and tamed is he;
but fat cat on the mat
　　kept as a pet,
　　he does not forget.

# The Naming of Cats

The Naming of Cats is a difficult matter,
It isn't just one of your holiday games;
You may think at first I'm as mad as a hatter
When I tell you, a cat must have THREE DIFFERENT NAMES.
First of all, there's the name that the family use daily,
    Such as Peter, Augustus, Alonzo or James,
Such as Victor or Jonathan, George or Bill Bailey –
    All of them sensible everyday names.
There are fancier names if you think they sound sweeter,
    Some for the gentlemen, some for the dames:
Such as Plato, Admetus, Electra, Demeter –
    But all of them sensible everyday names.
But I tell you, a cat needs a name that's particular,
    A name that's peculiar, and more dignified,
Else how can he keep up his tail perpendicular,
    Or spread out his whiskers, or cherish his pride?
Of names of this kind, I can give you a quorum,
    Such as Munkustrap, Quaxo, or Coricopat,
Such as Bombalurina, or else Jellylorum –
    Names that never belong to more than one cat.
But above and beyond there's still one name left over,
    And that is the name that you never will guess;
The name that no human research can discover –
    But THE CAT HIMSELF KNOWS, and will never confess.
When you notice a cat in profound meditation,
    The reason, I tell you, is always the same:
His mind is engaged in a rapt contemplation
    Of the thought, of the thought, of the thought of his name:
                His ineffable effable
                Effanineffable
Deep and inscrutable singular Name.

# Strays

Not homeless but classless. Two cats, one up a tree, one under it, move one poet to write a diamond-shaped poem about them; another looks at a king; another catches mice by breathing down their holes with cheese-scented breath. Tobermory talks, Tobias is dead, Boots has lost two legs, Celestino surpasses them all. And there is one item from a cat's aunt.

## When I Play with My Cat

When I play with my cat, who knows whether she is not amusing herself with me more than I with her?

From *Essays*

STEPHEN'S AUNTIE AVERIL

## In Memoriam

In loving memory of our dearest best beloved Stephen who passed over 29th June 1957, and our darling most beloved Fluffkins who joined our other dear ones on 23rd July 1972. Your little spirits are always with me. Auntie Averil

From the *In Memoriam column* of *The Cat* magazine, July/August 1974

## Two-Legged Cat

Old dot-and-carry-two, Boots the cat
Who's lost one front and one back leg
To a hay-mower, is not put out by that.
Chased by no dog, he's grown sleek and fat
On veteran's rights, while others have to beg.


JOHN GITTINGS (aged 8)

## A Cat

Silently licking his gold-white paw,
    Oh gorgeous Celestino, for
God made lovely things, yet
    Our lovely cat surpasses them all;
The gold, the iron, the waterfall,
    The nut, the peach, apple, granite
Are lovely things to look at, yet
    Our lovely cat surpasses them all.

# Epitaph

Here lies Tobias, our dear cat,
Who breathed his last upon the mat,
His death was due to cook's mistake
In giving him our processed hake.
The moral's plain. It is no treat
For pets to have what humans eat.

## YAMAMURA BOCHO

# Cat

The cat, though innocent tonight, allows
Its eyes, that sometimes drowse,
Sometimes to move in anguish. Idle cat,
Too self-contented to remember that
Sometimes the lights go out; too fat to care;
Too certain that the certain dark will wear
Of all rare stars yours starriest, most rare.

*Translated from the Japanese by Graeme Wilson*

# The Cat and the Bird

Tell me, tell me, gentle Robin,
What is it sets thy heart a-throbbing?
Is it that Grimalkin fell
Hath killed thy father or thy mother,
Thy sister or thy brother,
Or any other?
Tell me but that,
And I'll kill the Cat.

But stay, little Robin, did you ever spare
A grub on the ground, or a fly in the air?
No, that you never did, I'll swear;
So I won't kill the Cat,
That's flat.

GEOFFREY TAYLOR

# Cruel Clever Cat

Sally, having swallowed cheese,
Directs down holes the scented breeze,
Enticing thus with bated breath,
Nice mice to an untimely death.

# Tobermory Talks

. . . Miss Resker, in her best district-visitor manner, asked if the human language had been hard to learn. Tobermory looked squarely at her for a moment and then fixed his gaze serenely on the middle distance. It was obvious that boring questions lay outside his scheme of life.

'What do you think of human intelligence?' asked Mavis Pellington lamely.

'Of whose intelligence in particular?' asked Tobermory coldly.

'Oh, well, mine for instance,' said Mavis, with a feeble laugh.

'You put me in an embarrassing position,' said Tobermory, whose tone and attitude certainly did not suggest a shred of embarrassment. 'When your inclusion in this house-party was suggested Sir Wilfrid protested that you were the most brainless woman of his acquaintance, and that there was a wide distinction between hospitality and the care of the feeble-minded. Lady Blemley replied that your lack of brain-power was the precise quality which had earned you your invitation, as you were the only person she could think of who might be idiotic enough to buy their old car. You know, the one they call "The Envy of Sisyphus", because it goes quite nicely up-hill if you push it.'

Lady Blemley's protestations would have had greater effect if she had not casually suggested to Mavis only that morning that the car in question would be just the thing for her down at her Devonshire home.

Major Barfield plunged in heavily to effect a diversion.

'How about your carryings on with the tortoiseshell puss up at the stables, eh?'

The moment he had said it everyone realised the blunder.

'One does not usually discuss these matters in public,' said Tobermory frigidly. 'From a slight observation of your ways since you've been in this house I should imagine you'd find it inconvenient if I were to shift the conversation on to your own little affairs.'

The panic which ensued was not confined to the Major.

'Would you like to go and see if cook has got your dinner ready?' suggested Lady Blemley hurriedly, affecting to ignore the fact that it wanted at least two hours to Tobermory's dinner-time.

'Thanks,' said Tobermory, 'not quite so soon after my tea. I don't want to die of indigestion.'

'Cats have nine lives, you know,' said Sir Wilfrid heartily.

'Possibly,' answered Tobermory, 'but only one liver.'

'Adelaide!' said Mrs Cornett, 'do you mean to encourage that cat to go out and gossip about us in the servants' hall?'

The panic had indeed become general . . .

Even in a delicate situation like the present, Agnes Resker could not endure to remain too long in the background.

'Why did I ever come down here?' she asked dramatically.

Tobermory immediately accepted the opening.

'Judging by what you said yesterday to Mrs Cornett on the croquet lawn, you were out for food. You described the Blemleys as the dullest people to stay with that you knew, but said they were clever enough to employ a first-rate cook; otherwise they'd find it difficult to get anyone to come down a second time . . .'

From *Tobermory*

## Cats and Kings

With wide unblinking stare
   The cat looked; but she did not see the king.
She only saw a two-legg'd creature there
   Who in due time might have tit-bits to fling.

The king was on his throne.
   In his left hand he grasped the golden ball.
She looked at him with eyes of bright green stone
   And thought, *what fun if he should let it fall.*

With swishing tail she lay
   And watched for happy accidents, while he,
The essential king, was brooding far away
   In his own world of hope and memory.

O, cats are subtle now,
   And kings are mice to many a modern mind;
And yet there throbbed behind that human brow
   The strangely simple thoughts that serve mankind.

The gulf might not be wide;
   But over it, at least, no cat could spring.
So once again an ancient adage lied.
   The cat looked; but she never saw the king.

## A Cat's Example

For three whole days I and my cat
Have come up here, and patiently sat –
We sit and wait on silent Time;
He for a mouse that scratched close by,
At a hole where he sets his eye –
And I for some music and rhyme.

Is this the Poet's secret, that
He waits in patience, like this cat,
To start a dream from under cover?
A cat's example, too, in love,
With Passions's every trick and move,
Would burn up any human lover.

# Cat Musicians

One mixed blessing bestowed on human beings by cats is their music. It is said that their mewing contains sixty-three notes, and the name 'cats' melody' that we give to discordant sounds has arisen from the yowling and caterwauling that split the silence of moonlit nights.

The cat has always been connected with music and, perhaps because its body vibrates with deep purring, with musical instruments. It is, of course, by nature a player – as dragonflies, mice and birds know to their cost. A legend explains that the first cat was an offspring of the union of a lion and a monkey, and that it was from the monkey it inherited its playfulness.

No one seems to know why the cat is specially associated with fiddles. It may be something to do with the fact that the strings of violins are made of so-called 'cat-gut', a tough cord which is made from the intestines of animals, but it is usually taken from sheep and never from cats. No satisfactory explanation has been given as to why violin-strings should ever have acquired this name. The word may possibly be a corruption of 'kit-gut', 'kit' being an old word for a small fiddle.

Cat-orchestras have been a popular subject among illustrators of children's books, who frequently depict cats conducting, singing and playing every kind of instrument. At one time there were people who dressed up cats and exhibited them as 'musicians'. The last public cat-concert appears to have been given by a Venetian in London in 1789.

In the fifteenth century, the terrible cat-organs were invented. Twenty cats would be confined in narrow cases in which they were unable to move. Their tails, which protruded, were tied by cords attached to the keyboard of the organ, so that when the keys were pressed the cords were raised and the cats' tails pulled to make them mew. Later this organ was improved on, and various other instruments were constructed whose music was provided by tortured cats. It is difficult to understand how the cries of suffering animals could have been found entertaining by people for several centuries.

No one who has observed the luxuriating sensuality of a cat can doubt that it is a pleasure-loving animal. The grace and co-ordination of its movements are only equalled, in the human sphere, by dancers. But the only time a cat can strictly be said to dance is on those occasions when it prances around and leaps in the air, apparently partnered by a ghost though in fact by an unseen insect.

A bas-relief in a Roman museum shows a woman playing a lyre and trying to teach a cat to dance. She has hung two dead birds from a branch just above the cat's head, so that it prances about on its hind legs. . . .

From *Cult of the Cat*

# Lines of Reproach to a Cat on a Wall

Good cat, you do protest too much;
Why should my amiable touch
Arouse you to such mad alarm?
Surely you see I meant no harm?
It was a mild discreet caress;
Why then contort yourself and hiss
As though I were a fiend from Hell?
Surely you know I meant you well?

Consider yourself lucky that
You're not a mediaeval cat.
Our forebears would have smelt perdition
In your frenetic exhibition.
It would have led them to conclude
That you were one of Hecate's brood,
Familiar to the Evil One
And some emaciated crone,
And you'd have been hanged, burned, or hacked
In reeking particles.
                                    In fact
I would have disapproved of this;
I never do condone excess
Of any nature.
                                    All the same,
You'd only have yourself to blame.

## Cat-Faith

As a cat, caught by the door opening,
on the perilous top shelf, red-jawed and raspberry-clawed,
lets itself fall floorward without looking,
sure by cat-instinct it will find the ground
where innocence is; and falls
anyhow, in a furball, so fast that the eye
misses the twist and trust
that come from having fallen before,
and only notices cat silking away,
crime inconceivable in so meek a walk,

so do we let ourselves fall morningward
through shelves of dream. When, libertine at dark,
we let the visions in, and the black window
grotesques us back, our world unbalances.
Many-faced monsters of our own devising
jostle at the verge of sleep, as the room
loses its edges and grows hazed and haunted
by words murmered or by woes remembered,
till, sleep-dissolved, we fall, the known world leaves us,
and room and dream and self and safety melt
into a final madness, where any landscape
may easily curdle, and the dead cry out . . .

but ultimately, it ebbs. Voices recede.
The pale square of the window glows and stays.
Slowly the room arrives and dawns, and we
arrive in our selves. Last night, last week, the past
leak back, awake. As light solidifies,
dream dims. Outside, the washed hush of the garden
waits patiently, and, newcomers from death,
how gratefully we draw its breath!
Yet, to endure that unknown night by night,
must we not be sure, with cat-insight,
we can afford its terrors, and that full day
will find us at the desk, sane, unafraid –
cheeks shaven, letters written, bills paid?

# Diamond Cut Diamond

Two cats
One up a tree
One under the tree
The cat up a tree is he
The cat under the tree is she
The tree is wych elm, just incidentally.
He takes no notice of she, she takes no notice of he.
He stares at the woolly clouds passing, she stares at the tree.
There's been a lot written about cats, by Old Possum, Yeats, and Company,
But not Alfred de Musset or Lord Tennyson or Poe or anybody
Wrote about one cat under, and one cat up, a tree.
God knows why this should be left to me
Except I like cats as cats be
Especially one cat up
And one cat under
A wych elm
Tree.

# Cat-Lovers and Cat-Haters

The people who hate cats are quite an interesting group of people, and I have created a little rogues' gallery of cat haters so that you will be able to pick their counterparts out from among your friends (if you do not have a cat to do this for you).

The most unusual type of cat hater is the person who hates them because he is terrified of them. They have a long name for this. But for the life of me I can't remember it. However, it is something or other ending in phobia. I don't pretend to know how one catches this phobia, nor even if it is contagious, nor what will get rid of it.

There is also a group of people whose hobbies contrast rather violently with those of the cat. These people are only anti-catters part of the time, but they make up for this part-time occupation by the vigour with which they pursue it.

Mice are also anti-catters, and of course for the best reason. The only time they get the better of the cat is in cartoons, or other comic situations, including any dreaming they may do.

Some people are anti-catters for reasons of health. The majority of these are simply allergic to cats. They may not even know a cat is around until their radar-like noses inform them of the fact. Too bad they aren't allergic to submarines or pickpockets. The remainder of this group who believe cats can influence health live, for the most part, in lion, tiger or leopard country. They believe life can be considerably shortened by the presence of a very large, mean and hungry beast. A few rabid anti-catters go so far as to say that hungry or not, the lion, tiger, leopard or whatnot will eat you on general principles or just to keep his hand in.

Dictators, who are simply do-it-yourself kings of questionable ancestry and unspeakable table-manners, don't as a rule, like cats. At bottom it is just that dictators find the independent air in the cat quite intolerable. Freedom is the very last thing a dictator wants to have on his mind. This has led some scholars, cartoonists, foreign correspondents, etc., to the conclusion that dictators are related to certain rodents that don't like cats either. Thus dictators don't like cats because cats don't like them.

Now, happily, we come to the cat lover. He will have one cat on tap at all times, and maybe more. However, the genuine cats-come-first-people-come-second type of cat lover will tell you that you don't even get into the club unless you have at least four. Now you may say four cats are all right, but by four cats are meant four very fertile cats with full permission to let nature take its course. Cat lovers can readily be identified without any assistance from us. No matter what they wear, their clothes always look old and well used. Their sheets look like bath towels, and their bath towels look like a collection of knitting mistakes.

Undoubtedly the most unusual cat lover is the individual who, upon deciding he can't stand his relatives and what the hell he can't take it with him, chooses to leave everything to his cat, Tobermory. This poses an interesting problem, for cats, intelligence notwithstanding, do not have the necessary equipment to endorse the numerous cheques involved. True, they can be admirably employed in cancelling their cheques with their teeth. For this reason cats have to have trustees down at the bank, which is about the only time that people really get to know exactly what it is like to be employed by a cat.

From *How to Live with a Calculating Cat*

# Acknowledgments

HILAIRE BELLOC, 'A Conversation With A Cat' from *A Conversation With a Cat and Others* reprinted by permission of A. D. Peters and Co. Ltd.

N. MARGARET CAMPBELL, extract from *The Undoing of Morning Glory Adolphus* by permission of Hawthorn Books.

ELIZABETH COATSWORTH, 'On a Night of Snow' from *Night and the Cat*. Copyright Elizabeth Coatsworth. By kind permission of Mark Paterson on behalf of Elizabeth Coatsworth.

RICHARD CHURCH, 'The Cat' from *Collected Poems* by permission of the Estate of the late Richard Church, Laurence Pollinger Ltd and William Heinemann Ltd.

COLETTE, 'The Long Cat' from *Creatures Great and Small*, translated by Enid McLeod, by permission of the author, translator and Martin Secker & Warburg Ltd.

W. H. DAVIES, 'A Cat's Example' from *The Complete Poems of W. H. Davies* by permission of Mrs H. M. Davies and Jonathan Cape Ltd.

ALAN DIXON, extract from *Cat In the Long Grass* by permission of The Charles Skilton Publishing Group.

CLIFFORD DYMENT, 'Man and Beast' from *Axe In the Wood* by permission of the author and J. M. Dent & Sons Ltd.

PATRICIA DALE-GREEN, extract from *Cult of the Cat* by permission of the author and William Heinemann Ltd.

T. S. ELIOT, 'Skimbleshanks the Railway Cat' and 'The Naming of Cats'. Reprinted by permission of Faber & Faber Ltd from *Old Possum's Book of Practical Cats* by T. S. Eliot.

ELEANOR FARJEON, 'Cat' from *Poems For Children*. Reprinted by permission of Harold Ober Associates Inc. Copyright 1938 by Eleanor Farjeon. Renewed 1951.

ROY FULLER, 'The Family Cat' from *Collected Poems 1936–1961* by permission of the author and André Deutsch Ltd.

ROBERT GRAVES, 'Cat Goddesses' from *The Collected Poems 1975* by permission of the author and A. P. Watt & Son Ltd.

ERIC GURNEY, extract from *Cat Lovers and Cat Haters*, by permission of the author and W. H. Allen & Co. Ltd.

MICHAEL HAMBURGER, 'The London Tomcat' from *Flowering Cactus* by permission of the author.

TED HUGHES, 'Of Cats' and 'Esther's Tomcat'. Reprinted by permission of Faber & Faber Ltd from *Lupercal* by Ted Hughes; extract from 'How the Cat Became', reprinted by permission of Faber & Faber Ltd from *How the Whale Became* by Ted Hughes.

PAUL JENNINGS, 'Ailurophobe and Ailurophile' by permission of Concertina Publications Ltd.

BRIAN JONES, 'Death of a Cat' from *Poems, A Family Album* by permission of the London Magazine.

MICHAEL JOSEPH, extract from *Charles – The Story of a Friendship* by permission of Mrs Michael Joseph and Michael Joseph Ltd.

IRVING LAYTON, extract from 'Cat Dying in Autumn' from *Collected Poems* by Irving Layton, reprinted by permission of The Canadian Publishers, McClelland and Stewart Limited, Toronto.

VACHEL LINDSAY, 'The Mysterious Cat'. Reprinted by permission of Macmillan Publishing Co. Inc. from *Collected Poems* by Vachel Lindsay. Copyright 1914 by Macmillan Publishing Co Inc., renewed 1942 by Elizabeth C. Lindsay.

LOUIS MACNEICE, 'The Death Of a Cat'. Reprinted by permission of Faber & Faber Ltd from *The Collected Poems of Louis MacNeice*.

DON MARQUIS, extract from *The Tom Cat*, by permission of Doubleday & Co. Inc.; 'The Song of Mehitabel', reprinted by permission of Faber & Faber Ltd from *Archy and Mehitabel* by Don Marquis.

EWART MILNE, extract from *Diamond Cut Diamond* by permission of The Bodley Head.

MARIANNE MOORE, 'Peter'. Reprinted by permission of Faber & Faber Ltd from *The Complete Poems of Marianne Moore*.

MERRILL MOORE, 'Why He Stroked the Cats' from *Poems* by permission of Ann Leslie Moore.

HAROLD MUNRO, 'Milk for the Cat' and 'Catsmeat' from *The Collected Poems of Harold Munro* by permission of the author and Gerald Duckworth & Co. Ltd.

ALFRED NOYES, 'Cats and Kings' from *Collected Poems* by permission of John Murray (Publishers) Ltd.

RUTH PITTER, 'Mister the Blitzkit' and 'Quorum Porum' from *Collected Poems* by permission of Barrie & Jenkins.

ALASTAIR REID, 'Cat-Faith' from *Oddments, Inklings, Omens, Moments* by permission of the author.

E. V. RIEU, 'The Lost Cat' and 'Cat's Funeral' from *Collected Poems* by permission of Michael Rieu.

DOROTHY L. SAYERS, 'War Cat' from *Lords of Life* by permission of David Higham Associates Ltd.

IAN SERRAILIER, 'Miss Tibbles' and 'Death of the Cat' from *Poems* Copyright 1950 Ian Serrailier, by permission of the author.

STEVIE SMITH, 'The Singing Cat' and 'Monsieur Pussycat, Blackmailer' from *The Collected Poems of Stevie Smith* by permission of the Executor of the Estate of the late Stevie Smith, James MacGibbon.

LYTTON STRACHEY, 'Cat' from *The Cambridge Review* by permission of The Society of Authors as agents for the Strachey Trust.

A. S. J. TESSIMOND, 'Cats' from *Selection* by permission of the Literary Executor of the Estate of the late A. S. J. Tessimond, Hubert Nicholson.

RUTHVEN TODD, 'Two-legged Cat' from *Garland for the Winter Solstice* by permission of the author and J. M. Dent & Sons Ltd.

J. R. R. TOLKIEN, 'Cat' from *The Adventures of Tom Bombadil* by permission of George Allen & Unwin (Publishers) Ltd.

PAUL VALERY, 'White Cats', translated by David Paul, by permission of Routledge and Kegan Paul Ltd.

P. G. WODEHOUSE, extract from *The World of Mr Mulliner* by permission of Barrie & Jenkins.